THE COMPLETE

Trailering
Your Boat

THE COMPLETE GUIDE TO
Trailering
Your Boat

How to Select, Use, Maintain, and Improve a Boat Trailer

BRUCE W. SMITH

International Marine / McGraw-Hill

Camden, Maine • New York • Chicago • San Francisco • Lisbon • London • Madrid
Mexico City • Milan • New Delhi • San Juan • Seoul • Singapore • Sydney • Toronto

The McGraw·Hill Companies

1 2 3 4 5 6 7 8 9 DOC DOC 0 9 8 7

Library of Congress Cataloging-in-Publication Data
Smith, Bruce W., 1944–
    The complete guide to trailering your boat : how to select, use, maintain, and improve a boat trailer/Bruce W. Smith.
        p.   cm.
    Includes index.
    ISBN 978-0-07-147164-0 (pbk. : alk. paper)
    1. Boat trailers.   I. Title.
    GV775.S56 2007
    797.1'24—dc22   2007038397

ISBN 978-0-07-147164-0
MHID 0-07-147164-2

Questions regarding the content of this book should be addressed to
International Marine
P.O. Box 220
Camden, ME 04843
www.internationalmarine.com

Questions regarding the ordering of this book should be addressed to
The McGraw-Hill Companies
Customer Service Department
P.O. Box 547
Blacklick, OH 43004
Retail customers: 1-800-262-4729
Bookstores: 1-800-722-4726

Unless otherwise noted, all photographs by the author. Page ii by *Trailer Boats*.

1

Introduction

Becoming a boatowner can be one of the most gratifying and exciting events in life. Boats bring a sense of freedom and well-being in a way few other possessions can. Boats enable us to escape the pressures of the everyday world through fishing, waterskiing, or the simple act of a peaceful cruise. Add the companionship of friends and family, and you have a recipe for a rich, healthy lifestyle that you can pass on to your children and grandchildren.

I know because that's how my dad looked at boating and boatownership—and it's how I feel when there's a boat parked in my driveway.

But along with those feelings of gratification and joy come new responsibilities and tough decisions. They begin even before you slide your boat into the water for the first time, or take your first boating safety class. From the moment you decide to buy a boat, you're faced with the question of how to transport it. And since more than 95 percent of all recreational boats in the United States are trailerable, it's a question that applies to the majority of boaters.

THE CHALLENGES OF TOWING

Trailering, or towing, a boat imposes several challenges: selecting the right towing equipment; driving safely; and launching and retrieving the boat on a slippery boat ramp, all while other boaters wait their turn and look on critically. Responsible boatowners understand that meeting these challenges is just as important as handling a boat safely and courteously on the water.

I know firsthand the misfortunes that can befall a boatowner when it comes to towing. During one trip, I looked in the side mirror and saw a trailer tire and wheel rolling off to the side of the highway, and, a moment later, realized the wheel belonged to me.

Another time, I towed a friend's boat that was, as I later learned, much too heavy for my vehicle. I nearly lost control when a gust of wind hit my rig as I crossed over a long, high bridge. That time, I was lucky, but in that kind of situation, you don't want to depend on luck.

Less-dramatic learning experiences can also make you better at towing a boat. Picture a busy Saturday morning at your local boat ramp, and you're jockeying your trailer back and forth, trying to line it up on the ramp. Meanwhile the

Choosing the right towing equipment, and learning how to use it, are challenges faced by all boatowners, regardless of the size of their boats and tow vehicles.

boaters behind you are giving you the evil eye while they have to wait to launch their boats. Such an experience can be a real motivator toward improving trailering skills.

Sure, experiencing the consequences of such mistakes will help you avoid them in the future, but you can learn just as much secondhand. Why not learn from someone else's mistakes? Whether you're a complete newcomer to trailering or you've had one too many launch-ramp disasters, this book is for you. If you take it slow and devote a bit of time to learning the basics, then practicing the procedures as described, you'll soon acquire the skills to make trailering just another aspect of boating—something to approach prudently, but without undue worry.

DEVELOP A BASE OF KNOWLEDGE

To tow safely and effectively depends on many factors, most of which are elemental in their simplicity, yet critical when taken as a whole. For example, having your tow vehicle equipped with the right towing equipment and proper drive-train components is not sufficient in and of itself. Neither is keeping your tow vehicle in top condition, selecting the right hitch and trailer, or properly equipping and maintaining them. However, put them all together, and they become the foundation for safe towing.

The base of essential knowledge extends far beyond just buying and maintaining hardware. Knowing how to use it is equally important. This includes topics such as preparing and securing the boat for towing, hitching the trailer to the tow vehicle, and driving the rig. Whether you're on the open road or on congested city streets, towing is different from driving around sans trailer. While not difficult to learn, the special driving skills are essential.

The same holds true for the launching and retrieving skills you'll need at the boat ramp. This is where you'll reveal your true level of towing prowess—where other boaters watch everyone else's moves, good and bad. I want you to be a shining example of a boatowner who really knows the fine points of trailering.

Learning how to tow any trailer can be a bit overwhelming. So we're going to break it down into simple components: the tow vehicle, the trailer hitch, the boat trailer, the boat, and last, but not least, you.

The Tow Vehicle

One of the most common misconceptions is that any vehicle with a tow ball or a trailer hitch can tow just about anything. Nothing could be further from the truth. Every vehicle has specific limits on what it can safely tow. In Chapter 2, we'll cover these limitations and why they are important to your safety and to that of others who share the road with you.

You'll also find a lot of advice about choosing a good tow vehicle. You may have your heart set on a nice car to tow your boat, but as we shall see, you probably should set your sights on a pickup or SUV. Various pros and cons apply to every type of vehicle, involving trade-offs in towing capacity and ease, passenger room and comfort, fuel economy and power, reliability and durability, as well as other factors. You'll have to decide whether you'll use your tow vehicle just for towing or also for your daily transportation needs. This may strongly influence whether you keep your existing vehicle or buy a new one.

The basic information in this book will help you make that decision and also get the most for your dollar if you do buy new. I'll lead you through the vehicle selection process, including options that will make towing easier and safer.

Trailer Hitches

Once we've explored the tow vehicle, we'll delve into the details of trailer hitches in Chapter 3. Such a topic may sound boring at first, but understanding hitches and hitch ratings is crucial to everything towing related.

There are five classes of hitches, and each class has specific limitations regarding the weight it can safely tow. Having the wrong hitch or overloading a hitch can result in disastrous consequences. That's a scary thought when you realize that many boatowners pay little to no attention to the weight of the boat on their hitch.

But you won't have to worry about such things. The information in these pages will help you make a well-educated decision in choosing the right hitch for your tow vehicle, trailer, and boat. To get started, and to make sense of several

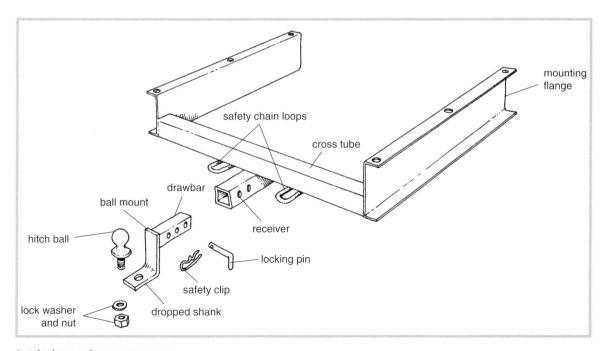

Basic hitch terminology. (CHRISTOPHER HOYT)

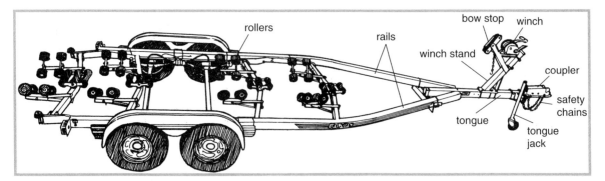

Basic trailer terminology. (JIM SOLLERS)

hitch-related references in the next couple of chapters, take note of the basic hitch terminology in the illustration on page 3.

Boat Trailers

In Chapter 4, we'll focus on boat trailers. At first glance, they may all look alike; however, as you read on, you'll discover they have many nuances. I'll show you how to (1) match a trailer to your boat, (2) choose the right trailer options, and (3) make sure the trailer is properly equipped for your particular boating needs.

To help with the terminology, the illustration above shows the basic components of a trailer and some optional accessories.

If you're a sailor, you'll have some special trailering considerations to take into account, so I've dedicated Chapter 7 to sailboats. In that chapter, we'll cover buying a trailer, positioning your sailboat on a trailer, launching and retrieving, and rigging issues.

Regardless of the type of tow vehicle and boat trailer you have, preventive maintenance is a key issue, both for safety and as a means of protecting your investment. I'll address both trailer and tow vehicle maintenance in Chapter 8.

The Boat

The boat is a huge factor in towing: its style, weight, beam, length, and height impose requirements on all the components related to the trailer, hitch, and tow vehicle. An owner towing a 12-foot aluminum jonboat that weighs 200 pounds will not have the same trailer and tow vehicle requirements as the one with an 8,000-pound, 26-foot cabin cruiser, or a 28-foot sailboat with a 5-foot-deep fixed keel. Each type of boat requires a different combination of towing components.

I will not address the boat in its own chapter because boat variables impact virtually every discussion related to the selection and use of the tow vehicle, hitch, and trailer.

Trailering Skills

Of course, the most crucial component of trailering is you, the driver. You are responsible for selecting the right towing equipment; making sure it's maintained and used correctly; driving appropriately; and knowing how to launch and retrieve—and practicing these skills until you can do them as easily as driving without a boat in tow.

Understanding the basics of towing a boat and taking the time to practice those skills will make you a more confident driver. A towing rig is a much bigger package than what you are probably accustomed to driving, requiring more concentration and attention to your surroundings, especially in the crowded conditions you are likely to find around the launch ramp.

In Chapter 5, we will discuss the art of towing, including how to prepare your rig for towing, drive in a variety of conditions, and back up smoothly and effortlessly. In Chapter 6, I'll lead you through several launching and retrieving procedures to accommodate the various conditions you might encounter at the boat ramp.

Once you become proficient in trailering your boat—and you will—you'll be able to approach towing with confidence and enjoyment, not trepidation.

LICENSE AND INSURANCE

To be a responsible operator, you must know the state laws and regulations regarding towing and its permits, licenses, registration, and insurance. For example, every state has a maximum allowable trailer width, usually 96 inches (8') or 102 inches (8'6"). If your boat's beam exceeds this limit, it's known as an *overwide*, and you may need special towing permits. To determine this and other requirements, contact the Department of Transportation (DOT), or other relevant agency, which handles vehicle regulations. Do this for each state in which you plan to travel. (These agencies are listed by state in Appendix B.)

While you don't need any special driver's license endorsements for towing boat trailers, you must register your trailer and have it inspected. Again, check with your home state's DOT for registration and inspection requirements.

You will also need to check your auto insurance policy to determine what it covers when you're towing the boat. Ask your agent for advice, but read the policy—it takes precedence over what anyone *tells* you.

Many boatowners think that because the typical auto insurance policy covers the boat and trailer, they don't need additional trailer insurance. Not so. Most auto insurance policies only cover the boat and trailer while you're towing them. Once you disconnect the trailer from the hitch, the coverage ends. Therefore, it is good to have a *hull and machinery policy*, which protects the boat, trailer, and equipment (such as outboard engines and bolt-on accessories) from physical damage that occurs while the boat is in storage, when you're launching and retrieving, or when it's on the water.

Before checking on boat trailer insurance coverage with your local agent, take a few minutes to check out other insurance sources to compare prices and coverages. Here are a few sources that may be helpful:

- Bass Boat Insurance, 800-476-5667, www.bass-boat-insurance.com
- BoatUS, 800-283-2883, www.boatus.com/insurance

- Foremost Insurance Group, 800-237-2060, www.foremost.com
- United Marine Underwriters, 800-477-7140, www.unitedmarine.net
- Voyager Marine Insurance, 800-342-4444, www.voyagermarine.com
- Progressive Insurance, 800-776-4737, www.progressive.com
- MetLife Insurance, 800-638-5433, www.metlife.com

Choosing Your Vehicle

When I was growing up on the Oregon Coast, my dad towed everything from livestock trailers and flatbed car haulers to the family travel trailer and bow-rider. He never paid much attention to what was in tow because the big one-ton Chevy pickup he'd bought at a U.S. Forest Service auction for just such purposes could pull whatever he clamped to the hitch ball.

The old Chevy was a perfect example of his "bigger is better" way of thinking. It was a stout beast. The rear spring pack seemed to be at least 6 inches thick, and with a V-8 engine and a four-speed manual transmission with a "granny low" for first, it could haul 2,000 pounds of gravel or hay in the bed and pull four tons on the hitch with little strain. Our 19-foot runabout, which probably had a towed weight of less than 3,500 pounds, wasn't much of a challenge for this truck, and Dad zipped that boat around the boat ramps and country roads as if he were towing air.

That's a far cry from what I see today. All too often what turns up at boat ramps are big boats towed by small cars and trucks that are clearly not rated to tow such loads. Some of the tow vehicles I see look a lot like a boat struggling to get up on plane—the stern low, bow high, and the driver struggling to stay on a straight course.

From a safety standpoint, that's not a good combination. A vehicle towing a load greater than its manufacturer rating is potentially dangerous. Any quick change in steering or braking could upset the whole package, with the boat, trailer, and tow vehicle ending up in a tangled mess in a ditch, or worse yet, tangling with other vehicles.

Boatowners need to keep that in mind, especially when stepping into the boat-towing world for the first time. Remember: Just because a vehicle has a hitch ball on the bumper doesn't necessarily mean it can safely tow your boat.

WHY CARS CAN'T TOW

Every vehicle manufacturer designs its vehicles to carry specific loads. Cars and minivans are ideally suited to carrying people, but that doesn't mean they make good tow vehicles. In fact, the days when big sedans and station wagons could tow as much as some full-size pickups haven't been with us since a gallon of gas cost a buck. Fewer than a dozen cars in production today can tow more than 1,500 pounds, and of those, only a handful can tow up to 3,500 pounds.

Too much boat on too little truck. Note how the truck's rear end is depressed, and its front end is too high. Trying to tow a too-heavy load can damage your tow vehicle and lead to accidents.

To put this in perspective, an outboard-powered, 18-foot bow-rider or well-equipped fiberglass bass boat has a trailered weight closing in on 3,000 pounds. To tow such a boat safely, you'll need to slide behind the wheel of an SUV or pickup.

Why? Because automotive technology has changed dramatically in the last couple of decades, with a great deal of development devoted to improved passenger safety, better fuel economy, a smoother ride, and crisper handling. To achieve these perfectly commendable goals, vehicle manufacturers have transitioned from rear-wheel drive (RWD) vehicles with their large V-8 engines to front-wheel drive (FWD) systems, with lighter engines and transmissions and smaller engine compartments—all of which have had unfortunate ramifications for reducing towing capabilities.

Front-Wheel Drive

Front-wheel drive dramatically improves a vehicle's handling and traction, thus improving safety when road and driving conditions deteriorate. With less mass and fewer components to turn, FWD is also more fuel efficient than RWD.

The drawback of FWD is that a system designed to be light and efficient and powerful enough to move a vehicle fully loaded with passengers and cargo is not necessarily powerful enough to pull a trailer.

Front-wheel drive is also far less effective in controlling trailer sway than rear-wheel drive. When sway gets out of control, the trailer moves the rear of the vehicle from side-to-side. The heavier the rear of a vehicle relative to its front, the more stable the trailer. With more than 50 percent of a front-wheel-drive car's weight over the front axle, that built-in stability no longer exists.

Front-wheel drive is also at a disadvantage at the boat ramp. Although FWD provides great traction on the road in poor weather, it doesn't perform so well on a boat ramp: the weight of the trailer on the rear of the vehicle transfers some weight off the front wheels, causing them to lose traction. In contrast, the weight of a loaded trailer will typically increase drive-wheel traction on a RWD vehicle.

Only a few passenger cars are truly capable of towing boats of substantial size. The full-size Ford Crown Victoria is limited to 1,500 pounds. This one is almost certainly overloaded.

Unibody Construction

Another innovation in modern car design that has resulted in reduced towing ability is the *unibody* platform, on which nearly every car is now made. The unibody is a rigid, sheet-metal shell, which does not have the separate, underlying steel frame or chassis that was standard in pre-1980s cars. On conventional full-size pickups and SUVs, however, steel chassis are still common. Vehicles with a strong chassis bolted to a separate body have greater lateral stability, making them less subject to sway than a similar vehicle with a unibody design. The additional braking and steering loads imposed by towing have less effect on them. And the separate chassis provides a strong mounting point for a trailer hitch—something lacking in most unibody vehicles.

Exceptions

There are some exceptions to these generalities. A few crossover SUVs, known as CUVs—including Honda's Ridgeline pickup, the 2008 Saturn Outlook, and the Buick Enclave—have been designed specifically as tow vehicles with built-in trailer anti-sway control. Despite their unibody construction, these vehicles can tow 4,500 pounds or more due to special reinforcements built into the unibody. They may also have more robust cooling and drivetrain components. (By the way, CUVs are predicted to soon overtake SUVs in sales volume.)

Engine

Then there's the engine issue. Today's car engines are designed to maximize fuel economy, an objective that leads to small-displacement, high-revving, multiple-cam, multivalve engines. These engines pack a lot of horsepower, but they lack low-end torque, and torque—more than horsepower—is what gets a load moving.

Cooling Components

Towing creates a lot of heat as the engine works to move the additional weight of a trailer and boat, and that heat needs to be removed from the engine and engine compartment. Big, efficient radiators, transmission coolers, and engine oil coolers are essential for heat removal when towing. The majority of today's cars don't have these heavy-duty cooling components, so their tow ratings have been reduced accordingly to prevent overheating.

Brakes

As cars became smaller and lighter, car brakes became smaller as well. Currently, they are sufficient for stopping the car's own weight and the load it's carrying but not necessarily an extra ton or more of boat and trailer.

Bottom Line

Today's state-of-the-art cars, while lighter, safer, higher-performing, and more fuel-efficient than cars of 30 years ago, are not up to the task of towing a boat and trailer combo that weighs more than 1,000 pounds. If you want to tow a boat these days, you are probably going to be happiest with a full-size pickup, SUV, or CUV.

When it comes to buying a vehicle to tow your new boat, look closely at the tow ratings specified in the owner's manual. The manufacturer's ratings are

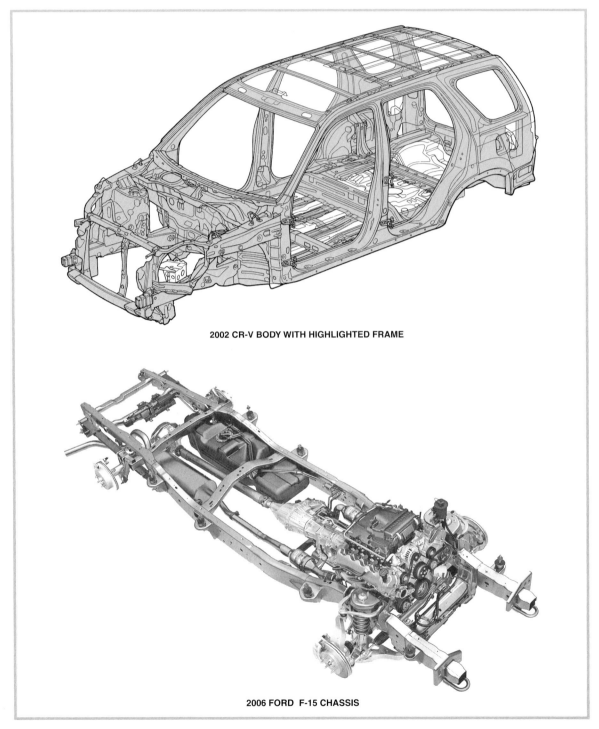

2002 CR-V BODY WITH HIGHLIGHTED FRAME

2006 FORD F-15 CHASSIS

Modern unibody vehicles (top) are light in weight, which improves fuel economy, but they lack the hefty frames of most full-size pickups and SUVs (bottom), which can bear more weight and provide strong attachment points for heavy-duty trailer hitches. (HONDA AND FORD MOTOR COMPANY)

derived from rigorous testing, and you expose yourself to potential danger—not to mention legal liability—if you tow a boat that exceeds your vehicle's rated capacity.

VEHICLE TOW RATINGS

Let's take a closer look at what these ratings mean. When an automotive manufacturer rates a vehicle's towing capacity at a certain limit, it means the vehicle will tow that weight anywhere in the country under any conditions. The air conditioner will work in Death Valley, and the brakes will work descending from the summit of Pike's Peak. The vehicle will pull that trailer along the Blue Ridge Mountains or across the desert to Lake Mead when the thermometer is holding steady at 115°F.

Tow a boat with a vehicle that is not rated for that load, however, and you run a risk of the vehicle breaking down. You are also placing yourself at risk—not just of personal injury and property loss, but of losing everything you have in a lawsuit should a towing accident involve other people. When you tow a trailer that weighs more than the upper limit established by either the vehicle or hitch manufacturer (whichever rating is lower), you assume all liability.

That's why tow ratings are far and away the most critical piece of the towing game. Unfortunately, those very ratings are the most confusing aspect of towing because of the many variables—even within a single vehicle model.

Weight-Carrying vs. Weight-Distributing

In most owner's manuals and towing guidelines, tow capacity ratings are divided into two categories: *maximum weight-carrying capacity* and *maximum weight-distributing capacity*. These two terms have totally different meanings, and understanding the differences is critical. It is also a source of controversy, as we will see below.

The *weight-carrying* (or deadweight) trailer-towing capacity is the maximum weight a vehicle can tow safely when the trailer is attached to the ball of a standard hitch receiver, which bears all the weight of the trailer's tongue. If you exceed that limit, you'll be placing too much weight on the rear of your vehicle, which will in turn lighten the front of the vehicle, which may adversely affect steering and control.

Similarly, the weight-carrying capacity inscribed on a hitch is the maximum weight the hitch manufacturer deems safe for towing with that particular hitch configuration. The limit on the hitch may be higher or lower than the limit on the vehicle—especially if you're purchasing a used vehicle whose previous owner installed the hitch. If the two ratings don't agree, *the lower of the two always takes precedence*.

The tow vehicle's *weight-distributing* trailer-towing capacity is the rating commonly referred to in advertisements and by salespeople. It's the maximum allowable weight that a vehicle can tow using a weight-distributing hitch assembly.

A weight-distributing hitch utilizes supplemental steel bars, called spring bars, attached between the trailer and the hitch receiver. These spring bars are adjusted with chains to distribute the weight of a heavy trailer more evenly across the tow vehicle's front and rear axles and those of the trailer, enhancing the rig's stability and handling characteristics. A vehicle's weight-distributing towing capacity will be higher than its weight-carrying towing capacity. The problem is that, while boats are rarely towed with weight-distributing hitches, for reasons that we'll discuss below, the distinction between the two ratings is largely ignored. The result is that a large percentage of boatowners focus mistakenly on the higher weight-distributing rating of their tow vehicle, and end up towing more than they should.

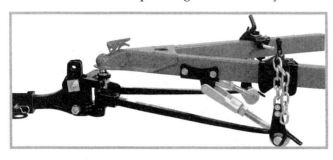

A weight-distributing hitch is designed to transfer part of the weight of the trailer to the tow vehicle's front wheels. (CEQUENT GROUP)

The weight-carrying trailer-towing capacity is the more relevant one for trailering a boat with the hydraulic surge brakes that come standard on most boat trailers. If you exceed that capacity, vehicle handling is compromised as is the durability of the drivetrain components. It may not break immediately, but the stress of overloading will cause accelerated wear on critical vehicle drivetrain components, leading to eventual mechanical failure. You also overburden the tow vehicle's braking system, overtaxing and overheating the brakes when negotiating long downhill stretches of road.

Tongue Weight

Listed or inscribed next to the maximum weight-carrying and weight-distributing ratings in a vehicle owner's manual or on a hitch, you'll note a second weight limit, the *maximum tongue weight (TW)*.

Tongue weight is the downward force of a trailer tongue on a hitch ball, and therefore on the rear of the tow vehicle, expressed either in pounds or as a percentage of the total weight of the tow (i.e., boat plus motor plus contents plus trailer). Again, this number has been derived by both the vehicle manufacturer and the hitch manufacturer as the safe limit for that product. Exceed that limit and you are, in racing terms, going beyond the redline.

Overload a hitch, for instance, and its mounting flanges could tear loose from the vehicle, or the cross tube or crossbar that supports the receiver tube could tear loose from the mounting flanges that anchor the hitch assembly to the vehicle frame. Too much TW could also shear the ball-mount platform or the threaded shank of the hitch ball itself.

While too much TW creates problems with the tow vehicle's handling, braking, and acceleration, too little TW, which induces trailer sway, is of even greater concern. As a Dodge towing guide stated, "Incorrect tongue weight could result in increased yaw or vehicle instability. A negative tongue weight could unload the rear suspension of the tow vehicle, decreasing vehicle stability."

The owner's manual for a tow vehicle will frequently state that a proper towing setup includes a TW that is 10 to 15 percent of the total tow weight. That's all well and good if you are towing a travel trailer, a couple of horses, or a trailer loaded down with ATVs or snowmobiles. But the 10 to 15 percent TW requirement doesn't work with most boat trailers.

Boat trailers are usually set up to have only 5 to 10 percent of the load on the hitch ball, because their longer trailer length, pole-tongue design, and fixed position of the load (boat) on the trailer makes them less prone to sway than their A-frame, box trailer brethren. The boat trailer's lower TW makes it easier to move the trailer around on its tongue jack when it's not hitched to the tow vehicle. But this is a secondary benefit; you should never modify the trailer's balance for this reason alone.

Manufacturer Tow Ratings and Boat Trailers

Perhaps surprisingly, vehicle tow ratings are not derived from any government formulas or regulations; they are not even standardized among auto manufacturers.

Each vehicle manufacturer has its own system for establishing tow ratings, which includes putting the vehicles through an intensive combination of highway and track testing with a box trailer in tow. Statistical data from the testing are combined with the impressions of the test drivers and the advice of corporate lawyers to establish the limits for a particular model when it is *properly equipped*.

Ah, *properly equipped*. Now those are two of the most powerful words in towing.

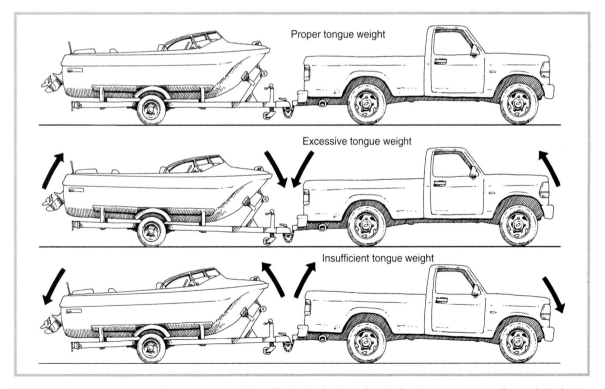

With the correct tongue weight (TW), the trailer and tow vehicle will be level and in line with each other (top). Too much TW will unweight the front wheels, reducing steering control (middle). Too little TW may cause trailer sway and, if there is negative TW, may reduce rear-wheel traction (bottom).

(PETER DUPRE/AUTOWORD, DRAWN BY CHRISTOPHER HOYT)

VEHICLE WEIGHT RATINGS

There are various limits to how much load your vehicle can carry safely. These include how much it can carry on each axle, the total combined weight it can carry, and how much it can tow. Each of these limits is important to vehicle durability and handling. Surpass any one of them and you put yourself, your passengers, and your vehicle at risk.

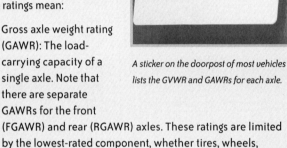

Automotive manufacturers provide this information in the form of gross weight ratings listed in the owner's manual, or on a placard inside the glove box or a doorpost. Here's what the ratings mean:

A sticker on the doorpost of most vehicles lists the GVWR and GAWRs for each axle.

- Gross axle weight rating (GAWR): The load-carrying capacity of a single axle. Note that there are separate GAWRs for the front (FGAWR) and rear (RGAWR) axles. These ratings are limited by the lowest-rated component, whether tires, wheels, springs, or the axle.
- Gross vehicle weight rating (GVWR): The maximum allowable loaded weight of a vehicle. This weight is the vehicle's curb weight plus the vehicle's maximum payload capacity plus the weight of the driver and passengers. Note that the GVWR may be lower than the sum of the GAWRs, since the safe operation of the vehicle depends upon more than just the carrying capacity of the axles. The brakes, for example, or even the engine's cooling capacity, might be the limiting factor.
- Combined gross vehicle weight rating (CGVWR): The maximum allowable loaded weight of a vehicle and the trailer it tows. In other words, it's the vehicle curb weight plus driver and passengers plus cargo plus loaded trailer weight.

Stay within the tow vehicle's maximum payload limits and its weight-carrying or weight-distributing towing limitations, and you'll never exceed any of the weight ratings placed on the vehicle. Pay extra attention to such ratings when towing a boat that weighs as much as or more than the vehicle itself.

These two words are the automotive version of a barbed-wire, electrified fence between towing with the full blessing of the vehicle manufacturer and fending for yourself if your vehicle breaks down while under warranty—or if you suddenly find yourself facing a wolf-pack of hungry liability lawyers after a towing accident.

A properly equipped vehicle has everything the manufacturer deems necessary to tow a certain load—everything from the proper engine and transmission to the correct axle ratio and related towing equipment, including the type of hitch being used.

It's interesting to dig into a vehicle manufacturer's towing guidelines. When you do such research, you'll frequently find (in the fine print of the owner's manual or at the end of a long series of notations in a towing brochure) an important stipulation: To achieve its maximum indicated tow rating, a vehicle must tow a trailer on a weight-distributing hitch (i.e., a hitch incorporating spring bars, also known as *weight-distributing bars*, or sometimes *load-equalizing bars*) and, in some cases, have sway-control or anti-sway devices between hitch and trailer as well. There's the rub for boatowners.

Those who tow conventional trailers—including travel trailers, horse trailers, car haulers, and utility and cargo trailers—only have to heed the limitations prescribed by both the vehicle and hitch manufacturer to tow in a safe, properly equipped manner. That typically means installing a weight-distributing hitch and adjusting the spring bars accordingly. The conundrum posed by boat trailers arises from the several factors that set them apart from other trailers.

Most states require all trailers over a certain weight (most commonly 3,000 pounds) to be equipped with brakes. This makes sense, since vehicle brakes are designed to stop the vehicle alone, not the additional

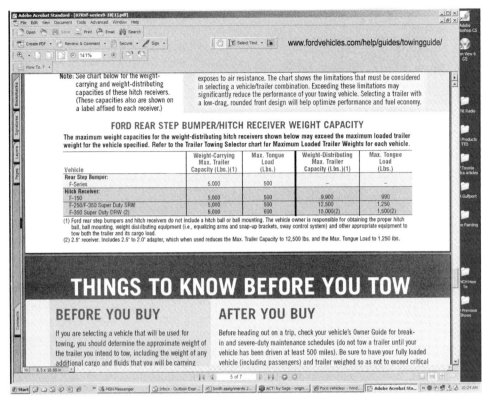

Vehicle manufacturers distinguish between weight-carrying and weight-distributing towing capacities and maximum TWs for their vehicles.

weight of a loaded trailer. Conventional (i.e., non-boat) trailers typically use *electric brakes*, which are activated by the same circuit that sends 12 volts to the tow vehicle's brake lights. Push on the vehicle's brake pedal, and you instantly engage the trailer brakes.

The majority of single- and tandem-axle boat trailers, on the other hand, use *hydraulic surge brakes* rather than electric brakes, because the latter are commonly considered to be vulnerable to immersion.

Surge brakes rely upon the forward movement of the trailer's tongue against the hitch ball to activate a hydraulic master cylinder inside the coupler. When the tow vehicle decelerates, the hitch ball pressing against this tiny brake cylinder activates the trailer's brakes, seamlessly working in concert with the tow vehicle's brakes to slow the entire tow package. (See Chapter 4 for more details on braking systems.) When the tow vehicle accelerates, pressure against the master cylinder is released and so are the brakes, just like taking your foot off the brake pedal in your car.

The dilemma is that the chain-attached bars of a weight-distributing hitch can potentially cause binding on the trailer coupler and interfere with surge-brake systems. If you install a weight-distributing hitch on a boat trailer equipped with surge brakes, you risk relying completely on the tow vehicle's brakes to bring your rig to a safe and efficient stop, and that's not a good situation from any perspective.

Boat trailer manufacturers say that the use of any device that impedes the function of their trailer's surge brake system places the user in the position of assuming all risks and liabilities related to the trailer's use. Representatives of both ShoreLand'r Trailers and EZ Loader Boat Trailers, the two largest manufacturers of boat trailers in the United States, say that boat trailers are not inherently set up for weight-distributing hitches, and they don't recommend such hitches on their trailers.

Another "properly equipped" caveat often noted in vehicle tow ratings is the requirement that trailers over a certain weight be equipped with sway-control devices. These rigid bars attach between the trailer tongue and the hitch on one or both sides to prevent or dampen the trailer's tendency toward side-to-side swaying. This caveat is not restricted to only heavy trailers. Towing guides for pre-2007, full-size Toyota pickups and SUVs, for example, say that sway-control devices are mandatory on trailers weighing more than 2,000 pounds. Likewise, Nissan's towing guide "strongly recommends" the use of a sway-control device for *all* of their pickups and SUVs when towing trailers weighing more than 2,000 pounds—and that includes just about any boat that's longer than 17 feet.

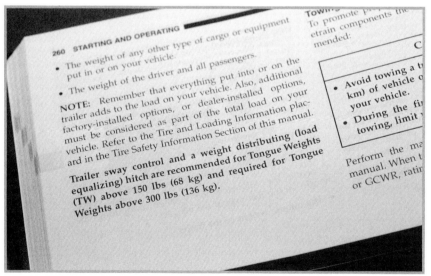

But sway-control devices are considered an absolute no-no by the manufacturers of boat trailers equipped with surge brakes, because while controlling sway, they also prevent any forward or backward movement between the hitch and the trailer, effectively rendering a surge-brake system inoperable.

The bottom line is that if you want to tow your boat within established factory guidelines, you can't use a weight-distributing hitch or a sway-control device on a trailer equipped with surge brakes, and you are therefore limited by the vehicle and hitch manufacturers' maximum *weight-carrying* towing recommendations.

Many automakers require sway-control devices for trailers above a certain weight, and they say so in their owner's manuals. Unfortunately, such devices are incompatible with most boat trailer brakes.

To keep your vehicle under warranty and avoid potential liability issues, *read the fine print*! Such research will probably reveal that the actual boat-trailer towing capacity of the vehicle you're looking at is as little as half its maximum factory tow rating, and maybe a lot less.

Even one of the biggest pickups out there, the two-wheel-drive, Cummins-powered Dodge Ram Mega Cab 3500, is limited in what it can tow in the weight-carrying mode. Although rated to tow 15,900 pounds with a weight-distributing hitch, the big Dodge can only tow 7,500 pounds with its weight-carrying factory hitch.

Similarly, Ford, a company that takes great pride in the towing ability of its trucks and SUVs, lists weight-carrying limits for many of its models that are far below the maximum trailer-towing capacities of those same vehicles utilizing a weight-distributing hitch system. For example, the 2006 Ford Explorer is limited to 5,000 pounds in weight-carrying mode, compared with 7,300 pounds using a weight-distributing hitch. The Ford F-Series pickups (F-150, F-250, and F-350) have 5,000-pound weight-carrying limits, even though some models have a weight-distributing towing capacity well in excess of 12,000 pounds.

The V-6-powered 2005 Toyota Tacoma is rated with a towing capacity of 3,500 pounds; 5,000 pounds when equipped with a Class IV hitch; and 6,500 pounds when equipped with Toyota's "Towing Prep Package," which consists of a Class IV hitch, transmission oil cooler, supplemental oil cooler, heavy-duty battery, 130 amp alternator, and seven-pin trailer plug socket with converter.

The Tacoma's tow ratings might appear to be higher than some of its competitors, but Toyota imposes a lot of caveats that reduce the attractiveness of some of its models as boat-towing vehicles. For example, deep in the 2005 Tundra owner's manual, you'll find such towing limitations as "not exceeding 45 mph when towing more than 1,000 pounds," and the necessity to use a "sway control device" when towing more than 2,000 pounds. Since you can't use an anti-sway control on a boat trailer with surge brakes, and since no one wants to turtle down the highway at 45 mph, such requirements are truly limiting.

The 2007 Toyota Tundra has one of the highest tow ratings in half-ton pickups. Yet all models with the V-8s require the use of a weight-distributing hitch when towing more than 5,000 pounds. And, all require sway-control devices for trailers weighing over 2,000 pounds.

Fortunately, there is a way out of the weight-carrying/weight-distributing rating dilemma for some boat trailers. Many of the larger trailers can now be equipped with electric or electric/hydraulic brakes as an optional upgrade, and these brakes are unaffected by weight-distributing hitches or sway-control devices. If your trailer has electric or electric/hydraulic brakes—and the trailer is designed to use a weight-distributing hitch—you can safely adhere to the maximum *weight-distributing* tow rating and tongue-weight guidelines set forth in your owner's manual. Adjust the weight-distributing hitch in the proper manner, and make sure the electric brakes and the tow vehicle's trailer wiring are in top shape before hitting the road.

In spite of their reputation for unreliability in the boating environment, electric/hydraulic brakes are, in fact, sufficiently reliable. Unfortunately, they are not common on trailers for boats smaller than about 26 feet and not available on most single-axle trailers. Additionally, for many trailers, they are often not available from the factory, even as an option. As the still-accepted norm for smaller

Table 2.1	TOW RATINGS FOR SELECTED VEHICLES			

Vehicle	Engine	Weight-Distributing Tow Capacity (with 150 lb. driver) (in pounds)	Max "Weight-Carrying" Capacity (with weight-carrying Class III hitch, or Class IV hitch without spring bars attached) (in pounds)	Tongue Weight (in pounds)
PICKUPS				
'06 Honda Ridgeline AWD	V-6	5,000	5,000	
'06 Dodge Dakota QC 4WD	V-8	6,926*	3,000	300
'06 Dodge Ram 2500 QC SB 2WD	V-8	12,000*	5,000	500
'05 Dodge Ram Power Wagon	V-8	11,000*	3,000	300
'06 Chevy Silverado CC Duramax 4×4	V-8	12,000*	7,500	1,000
'06 Toyota Tundra Double Cab 4WD	V-8	7,000*		200**
'07 Toyota Tundra DC 4×4	V-8	10,300	5,000	2,000
'06 Ford F-150 Crew Cab	V-8	9,200*	5,000	500
'07 Ford F-250 Crew Cab	Diesel	12,500	5,000	500
'07 Ford F-350 Dual Rear Wheel	Diesel	15,000	6,000	600
'06 Nissan Titan Crew Cab	V-8	9,400*	5,000	500
SUVS				
'06 Honda Pilot	V-6	4,500	4,500	
'06 Toyota RAV4	V-6	1,500	1,500 ***	
'06 Toyota Highlander	V-6	4,015**	2,000	
'06 Jeep Commander	V-8	7,150*	5,000	500
'06 Jeep Liberty 2WD	V-6	3,500*		300**
'06 Jeep Liberty 4WD Diesel	I-4	5,000*		300**
'07 Chevy Tahoe 4WD	V-8	7,700*	5,000	500
'06 Chevy TrailBlazer 2WD	I-6	6,300*	4,000	400
'06 Ford Explorer	V-8	7,300*	5,000	500
'06 Ford Escape	V-6	3,500	1,500	
'06 Nissan Pathfinder	V-6	6,000*	5,000	500
'06 Nissan Armada 2WD	V-8	9,100*	5,000	500

*Requires use of Class IV weight-distributing hitch and/or weight-distributing hitch with sway-control device.

**Requires use of sway-control device above this weight.

***Requires brakes on trailers weighing more than 600 pounds.

NOTES:

TW is considered part of the carried load on the vehicle, so for every 100 pounds added to the vehicle in passengers and cargo, you should deduct that weight from the maximum trailer weight the vehicle can tow.

Figures shown are representative and may not accurately reflect every vehicle so designated. Read your owner's manual and examine the hitch rating label to determine true capacities.

A complete list of maximum weight-distributing tow vehicle ratings for past and current vehicles can be found at www.trailerboats.com

boats, surge brakes are less expensive and, if you can sort out the tow rating issue, simpler to purchase.

Honda: An Exception to the Confusion

Automotive manufacturers are always pushing for a marketing edge, and tow ratings play a big role in that edge. Regardless of how small the difference is between two competing vehicles' tow ratings, the one with the bigger number is somehow perceived as being the better vehicle. Therefore, it's little wonder that clear-cut numbers are hard to ferret out. One of the few exceptions among vehicle manufacturers is Honda.

The mid-size Honda Ridgeline pickup lists a 5,000-pound maximum towing capacity with nary a mention of sway-control systems or weight-distributing hitches. Honda is also perhaps the most forthright manufacturer when it comes to assigning tow ratings to its smaller SUVs. Honda rates its Pilot and its MDX at 3,500 pounds for a box trailer and 4,500 pounds for a boat trailer—again with no caveats.

Honda is one of the few manufacturers—perhaps the only one—to openly differentiate between box trailers and boat trailers. A boat trailer has less wind resistance, so there's less load on the tow vehicle's cooling system. Another reason is that Honda engineers have noted differences in stability between the two types, especially when a semitruck passes or is passed by the tow vehicle.

Imagine you're passing a big rig on the highway. As your tow vehicle and trailer break through the truck's large pressure wake—the high-pressure area created in the front of the truck as it moves forward—you experience an immediate effect on vehicle handling and stability. As the trailer passes through the air wake, it experiences a significant sideways force, which tends to push the tow vehicle to the side. When that happens, the tow vehicle must be stable enough to keep both itself and the loaded trailer under full control. Because boat trailers have less surface area for wind to press against, it has more stability than a box trailer. Honda chassis engineers take this factor into consideration and set the boat-tow rating higher.

Honda, to its credit, has created clear, simple, easy-to-understand tow specifications. The Pilot and the MDX are rated to tow 4,500 pounds with four people in the car. The Ridgeline is rated at 5,000 pounds with two people in the truck. Most other automakers base their tow ratings on an assumption of only one person in the vehicle, and the user must adjust the towing rating accordingly.

The Future of Standardization

Towing would be a lot easier if the automakers could all agree on a standard basis for establishing tow ratings, and especially if they would supply separate ratings for boat trailers. Maybe someday we'll see that happen. In 2005, a group of towing engineers within General Motors (GM) helped set up a tow vehicle trailer rating subcommittee within the Society of Automotive Engineers International (SAE) in an effort to bring clarity and common sense to tow ratings.

According to GM trailering engineer Rob Krouse, one of the key engineers involved in this subcommittee, "Ultimately, the goal we are striving for is that when you see a 5,000-, 7,000-, or 15,000-pound trailer rating, it will mean the same whether it comes from Ford, GM, Chrysler, Toyota, Nissan, Honda, or any other vehicle manufacturer.

"We have reps from all of those companies in this subcommittee, along with representatives from RVIA (the Recreational Vehicle Industry Association, NATM (the National Association of Trailer Manufacturers), and indirectly from NMMA (the National Marine Manufacturers Association). As an industry, we're aware of these towing and tow-rating issues," said Krouse. "Hopefully, over the next few years, we'll come up with some semi-standardized rules—or at least guidelines that might clarify the tow rating situation."

You Can't Escape the Ratings

Trailer weight-capacity issues create some interesting towing calculations for boatowners, but the bottom line is this:

> When you're juggling weight-carrying, weight-distributing, tongue-weight, and hitch-capacity ratings, it's the lowest number that determines your vehicle's boat-towing limitation.
>
> Towing a trailer that exceeds that lowest weight figure places your rig outside safe towing parameters.

You can't work around a vehicle's weight-carrying limitations by upgrading to a stronger hitch, say from a Class III to a Class IV or V (we'll talk more about hitches in Chapter 3). The limit placed on the vehicle by the manufacturer is not necessarily due to the hitch's capacity. For example, handling problems that arise from overloading the back end of the tow vehicle could be the limiting factor.

If you're committed to towing your boat in a safe and liability-free manner, don't exceed the listed weight-carrying capacity of your tow vehicle if the trailer is equipped with surge brakes. On the other hand, if the boat you want to tow is sitting on a trailer equipped with electric or electric/hydraulic brakes, you can follow the maximum weight-distributing tow rating and tongue-weight guidelines set forth in your owner's manual. The provisions, of course, are that (1) you install a weight-distributing hitch, and (2) your trailer is capable of accepting such a hitch, either by design or with the use of an adapter (which may be required on many pole-tongue trailers).

For many first-time boatowners, choosing a tow vehicle is a lot like the old chicken-and-egg scenario: Do you buy a tow vehicle to match the boat of your dreams, or do you buy a boat to match the tow vehicle in your garage?

Either approach is fine as long as the tow vehicle is a good match for its trailered boat. To assess that match, you have to use the ratings—not the vehicle's power or size, the salesperson's word, or what the advertisements proclaim or portray. Take heed to what is stated in the owner's manual first, then to the rating listed on the hitch. Nothing else matters at this point.

What Can Your Vehicle Really Tow?

As noted above, the distinction between weight-distributing and weight-carrying rating is often ignored by boatowners, who commonly devote much of their attention to TW limits, because boat trailer TWs appear to be the easiest limit to adhere to. Since a boat trailer's TW should be 5 to 8 percent of total towed weight (compared to the 10 to 15 percent that is common with other styles of trailers), many boat trailers that exceed the vehicle's weight-carrying rating will fall within acceptable TW limits.

Let's look at a hypothetical example. Say your tow vehicle has a weight-carrying capacity of 5,000 pounds, a weight-distributing rating of 7,300 pounds, and a TW limit of 500 pounds (a fairly typical 10 percent of the deadweight rating). Can you tow a trailer whose total loaded weight is 7,000 pounds? Let's assume that the trailer has conventional surge brakes, and to make sure that the hitch doesn't represent a limitation, let's equip the tow vehicle with a weight-carrying Class IV hitch with a capacity of 10,000 pounds.

The TW of a properly set up boat trailer should be 5 to 10 percent of the trailer's total loaded weight—in this case, 350 to 700 pounds. As long as you keep your trailer set up with the TW at 7 percent (490 pounds) or less, you won't overload the back end of the vehicle, and steering, handling, and front-end braking should all be OK. From the manufacturer's weight-distributing rating of 7,300 pounds, we know that the vehicle has the necessary power and cooling capacity to pull the trailer's 7,000-pound weight. So even though you're exceeding the vehicle manufacturer's weight-carrying rating, things seem to be OK all around, right?

Not necessarily—your ambiguous conclusion ignores two very serious issues: liability and vehicle warranty.

If you are involved in an accident while towing a weight in excess of the manufacturer's guidelines, the legal system will almost certainly hold that against you, regardless of whether you were at fault in causing the accident, and whether or not the trailer's weight had anything to do with it. And if you tow a trailer in excess of the manufacturer's guidelines even once, the manufacturer will be

WATCH THE SALES PITCH!

Tow ratings are an important element of vehicle marketing hype, especially among pickups and SUVs, and anyone looking for the perfect vehicle to tow his or her boat can easily be led astray by a sales pitch. I have to admit that I can document this with an experience of my own.

Several years ago, I decided to replace my old Dodge Ram pickup with a midsized SUV that could tow my 4,800-pound boat/trailer package while giving me improved gas mileage. The Chevy TrailBlazer caught my attention. It took little effort for the salesman to convince me that the TrailBlazer's I-6 was more fuel-efficient than the big V-8 in my older Dodge, and that the 6,300-pound maximum towing capacity of the Chevy was way more than enough to tow my boat. I bit, he sold.

Two weeks later, I realized the salesman had been only half right: the fuel economy of the Chevy I-6 was indeed better than the Dodge V-8, but the TrailBlazer was less than optimal as a tow vehicle. A combination of the "new truck bug" and a smooth-talking salesman had blinded me to the TrailBlazer's factory tow ratings.

The maximum tow rating was indeed 6,300 pounds if the truck and trailer were equipped with a weight-distributing hitch, but the weight-carrying limit was only 4,000 pounds.

My tow package—including a surge brake–equipped trailer on a standard hitch receiver—exceeded the truck's weight-carrying capacity by 800 pounds, making my new SUV a very uncomfortable and unstable towing platform. Eventually I moved up to a full-size tow vehicle with a more appropriate weight-carrying tow rating, but all that drama and expense could have been avoided if I'd been just a little more observant.

Of course, even the closest attention to tow ratings won't tell you what you need to know unless you first know the weight of your tow package.

within its rights to declare your warranty void for failure of any drivetrain or suspension component—from the engine right down to the tires.

Even though tow vehicles in weight-carrying mode may be technically capable of towing heavier boat trailers than box trailers (because of the difference in tongue weight), manufacturers have yet to make that distinction in their tow ratings. Eventually this may change, and the automakers will probably publish separate tow ratings that separate boat trailers from all other types. But until that occurs, concern for safety and liability make it imperative that you abide by the guidelines stated in your owner's manual.

PICKING A TOW VEHICLE

Many people look forward to buying a new vehicle, and some people will use a new boat as a welcome excuse to buy the one they've been lusting after. Cool down and stay rational. This decision is more a question of math than desire. Calculating the real weight of your boat and trailer package is a critical first step in choosing a proper tow vehicle.

Figuring Towed Boat Weight

"Trailer loading and actual towed vehicle size, shape, and configuration can change towing dynamics dramatically," says John Tiger, Jr., one of the towing specialists with the Cequent Group (which includes the brands Draw-Tite, Reese, Hidden Hitch, Tow Power, Tekonsha, and Bulldog). "That's why everyone who tows needs to know what the boat/trailer package actually weighs."

You can't just look in a boat's sales brochure, because the numbers you need probably aren't going to be there. What most boatbuilders list in their specifications is the dry hull weight, which does not include the weight of the engine(s), fuel, water, options, accessories, gear, or the trailer on which the boat is being towed. Without those additional figures, you can't know the exact weight your vehicle will be towing.

For instance, the typical boat trailer can weigh anywhere from a couple hundred to a couple thousand pounds, depending on the style and size. Then you have to add in the weight of the boat, engine, fuel (gas weighs 6.1 lb./gal., diesel 7.1 lb./gal.), water (8.3 lb./gal.), and whatever gear and provisions are stored inside lockers and coolers. All that weight adds up in a hurry.

A friend of mine took his family's 24-foot Sea Ray Sundeck to have it weighed. He was shocked to find out the package weighed 6,950 pounds—just 50 pounds shy of the maximum weight-carrying capacity of the Class IV hitch on his Chevy Suburban. He had thought his boat and trailer package were closer to 5,500 pounds, giving him a big margin of safety for the Suburban's 6,000-pound *weight-carrying* tow rating.

So don't be shocked if you find out that the true towed weight of your boat and trailer package is far more than you thought. Boat manufacturers have a knack for keeping the rigged-and-ready-for-the-water weight of their products unpublished. It's not so much that they don't want buyers to know how much the boat/trailer package weighs; rather, there are so many variables that it would be hard to list all the combinations. So they publish dry hull weights instead, leaving the burden of doing the math on you.

Say you have your eye on a slick little 19-foot fish-and-ski. Its dry hull weight is listed at 1,750 pounds—not too bad—but let's look at the weight of everything else:

- The four-stroke, V-6 outboard: 500 pounds
- 30 gallons of fuel: 183 pounds
- 56-quart ice chest filled with ice, food, and drinks: 80 pounds
- Skiing and fishing gear and accessories: 100 pounds
- Your fancy tandem-axle trailer: 800 pounds

Take a look at the tables that follow to get a sense of what things weigh, then tow your boat with full tanks and gear to a public truck scale, and spend a couple of bucks on a weigh ticket. Vehicle scales are found on major highways, as well as at some building supply companies, trucking companies, and junkyards. (If you can't find one nearby, ask a local moving company—they use them frequently.) The figure on the weigh slip will erase any doubts about towed trailer weight. You'd be surprised how many people drastically underestimate the weight of their boat/trailer packages.

It's important to know the total weight of your boat, gear, and trailer. The easiest way to find out is to take the rig to a weigh scale.

The vehicle scale may reveal that your fish-and-ski's 1,750-pound dry hull has turned into a 3,400-pound tow package. To tow this package in a safe manner, you're going to need a tow vehicle with a minimum weight-carrying hitch capacity of at least 3,600 pounds. The reason for the additional weight is that vehicle tow capacities are generally listed with only the driver, and you must deduct 150 pounds from the listed tow rating per additional occupant.

That's not so bad, except that many of today's compact SUVs and CUVs are limited to maximum trailer weights of less than 3,000 pounds.

Another example: Say you own a full-size, four-door, four-wheel-drive Ford F-150 SuperCrew and see a beautiful 26-foot sport cruiser that would fit right in with the family's summer vacation plans. The dry weight of the boat is 7,500 pounds, and the ads say that particular Ford can tow 9,500 pounds. Most of us would immediately think that's more than enough. But as with the fish-and-ski, a close look at the weigh slip and the Ford's towing capacities will tell a different story.

The sport cruiser has an 84-gallon fuel tank and a 28-gallon water tank. Filled, these tanks bring the weight up to 8,244 pounds. Add in the weight of the tandem-axle trailer and the towed weight is now over 9,000 pounds. If you want the optional generator and canvas curtain set on board, add in another 250 pounds. And you haven't even begun to load it with provisions, fishing gear, or other accessories.

Table 2.2	TYPICAL BOAT WEIGHTS BY LENGTH AND TYPE (in pounds/kilograms)										
	Boat Length (in feet)										
Boat Type	10	11	12	13	14	15	16	17	18	19	20
Family-Pleasure					263/ 119	353/ 160	646/ 293	1,841/ 835	2,302/ 1,044	2,431/ 1,082	3,027/ 1,373
Fishing	142/ 65	175/ 79	429/ 194	615/ 279	673/ 305	700/ 312	814/ 369	1,665/ 751	1,525/ 691	1,824/ 827	1,968/ 893
Sailboat	92.8/ 42	101/ 46	185/ 84	225/ 102	285/ 129	302/ 137	565/ 256	605/ 274	902/ 704	1,125/ 510	1,149/ 521
Rowboat	102/ 46	115/ 52	123/ 56	125/ 57	128/ 58	135/ 61	145/ 66	152/ 70	160/ 72		
	Boat Length (in feet)										
Boat Type	21	22	23	24	25	26	27	28	29	30	
Family-Pleasure	3,066/ 1,390	3,594/ 1,630	4,447/ 2,017	4,522/ 2,051	4,714/ 2,138	5,365/ 4,233	5,842/ 2,649	6,456/ 2,928	7,944/ 3,603	8,172/ 3,706	
Fishing	2,105/ 955	2,342/ 1,062	2,802/ 1,270	2,893/ 1,312	3,251/ 1,474	4,205/ 1,907	4,538/ 2,058	5,896/ 2,694	6,689/ 3,022	7,183/ 3,258	
Sailboat	2,213/ 1,003	2,227/ 1,010	2,540/ 1,152	2,689/ 1,219	2,838/ 1,287	3,510/ 1,592	3,656/ 1,689	6,250/ 2,835	7,053/ 3,199	7,290/ 3,307	

NOTE:
Weights are approximate hull weights, excluding engines, supplies, and accessories, and vary greatly from manufacturer to manufacturer and with the material of construction and design of each boat.
(Peter duPre/Autoword)

Meanwhile, the maximum tow rating for a properly equipped 2006 F-150 SuperCrew 4x4 with a 5.4-liter, V-8 engine and a 3.55:1 axle ratio—a common ratio in F-150s—is 8,200 pounds. The tow rating jumps to 9,200 pounds if the axle ratio is 3.73:1, but there's a catch. The 9,200-pound tow rating only applies in this case to the two-wheel drive (2WD) SuperCrew, not the four-wheel drive (4WD) version. It's common for 2WD trucks and SUVs to have a higher towing capacity than their 4WD counterparts. A 4WD weighs more, and that extra weight has to be deducted from the vehicle's CGVWR, which includes the weights of the tow vehicle and the trailer.

In addition, Ford requires the use of a Class IV *weight-distributing* hitch system to tow the maximum load—not the Class III hitch, rated to carry only 5,000 pounds, which the stock 2006 F-150 was set up with from the factory.

As we've already seen, however, a weight-distributing hitch will interfere with or disable a boat trailer's surge brakes, and towing a boat trailer without fully functioning brakes poses a serious safety concern. The end result of this analysis is that the 2006 F-150 is not suited to towing the big sport cruiser. Neither

Table 2.3	TYPICAL OUTBOARD ENGINE WEIGHTS BY HORSEPOWER (in pounds/kilograms)	
Engine Size (hp)	**2-Stroke Engines**	**4-Stroke Engines**
2		28/13
2.5	28/13	35/16
3	28/13	38/17
4		51/23
5	45/20	57/26
6		69/31
8	60/27	99/45
9.9	75/34	102/46
15	77/35	113/51
20		137/62
25	106/48	148/67
30		170/77
40	204/93	218/99
50	189/86	232/105
60	219/100	277/126
70	228/103	293/133
75	303/137	362/164
90	298/135	371/168
115	350/159	439/199
130		485/220
135	431/195	460/209
150	461/210	487/221
175	475/215	497/226
200	479/218	548/247
225	479/218	563/256
250	479/218	578/262
300	543/247	580/263

(Peter duPre/Autoword)

NOTE:
Weights are approximate dry weights and vary by manufacturer.

Table 2.4	TYPICAL WEIGHTS OF BOAT GEAR & SUPPLIES (in pounds/kilograms)				

Gear and Supplies	Typical Total Weights				
	Capacity				
	5 gal.	**10 gal.**	**20 gal.**	**30 gal.**	**40 gal.**
Water	42/19	83/38	167/76	250/114	339/151
Gasoline	31/14	62/28	124/56	186/84	248/112
Engine Oil	35/16	70/32	140/63	210/95	
	Boat Lengths				
	20 ft.	**21–25 ft.**	**26–30 ft.**	**over 30 ft.**	
Anchor Line with Chain	14/6	20/9	34/15	60/27	
Anchor	10/4	15/7	18/8	21/10	
	Number of Batteries				
	1	**2**	**3**		
Marine Starting Battery	41/19	82/38	123/57		
Trolling Motor Battery	60/27	120/54	180/81		

(Peter duPre/Autoword)

Table 2.5	MORE WEIGHTS OF BOAT GEAR & SUPPLIES (in pounds/kilograms)

Accessory	Weight
Electric Trolling Motor	10–35/4–15
Fishing Rod and Reel	2/1
Life Jacket	4/2
VHF Radio and Fish Finder	5/2
36 qt. Cooler with Ice	15/7
Sleeping Bag	4/2
Tent	7/3
Portable Radio/CD Player	8/4
First-Aid Kit	2/1
12-volt TV/VCR	20/9
Fire Extinguisher	10/4
Cookware	14/6
Dishes/Cutlery for 4 Persons	12/5
A Weekend's Food for 4 Persons	40/18

(Peter duPre/Autoword)

is an F-250 or F-350, unless the trailer is equipped with a weight-distributing hitch, and that means that you can't use surge brakes. You'll have to upgrade to hydraulic-electric brakes.

Before buying a new tow vehicle, know the weight of your tow package and the real towing capacity of the vehicle you have your eye on. Look for a vehicle with a maximum towing capacity at least 10 to 25 percent greater than the towed weight. That leaves you a margin of safety and alleviates the stress on your tow vehicle. Pushing a vehicle to its towing limit puts a tremendous strain on the engine, brakes, and transmission, potentially shortening the life of all those components.

Not only does the vehicle you choose have to be designed to tow the load, it also has to fit your lifestyle. There are literally thousands of combinations when it comes to tow vehicle choices. Cars, as mentioned earlier, are all but out of the picture unless the boat is very small and light. Fortunately pickups, SUVs, and CUVs happen to be the most popular vehicles on the road, accounting for more than half the new vehicles sold during the past few years. They also offer a long list of options and combinations that can make life on the towing road a very pleasant one.

Pickups

When it comes to choosing a pickup begin by determining which cab style best suits you.

Regular-cab pickups are a great choice if cost is your primary concern. Such models make great work trucks and provide maximum load-carrying and trailer-towing capabilities when ordered with a long bed and 2WD. Regular-cab models with short beds, on the other hand, are easier to maneuver in tight quarters and may fit the typical two-car garage.

However, interior room can be tight, with seating for three adults being cramped and behind-the-seat storage limited. If you want to maximize interior roominess, stay with the full-size offerings, such as the Dodge Ram, Toyota Tundra, Nissan Titan, Ford F-Series, or GMC/Chevrolet pickups. Be aware, too, that the resale value of a standard or regular-cab pickup is not that great when compared with extended-cab and four-door models.

Extended-cab pickups have clear advantages over regular cabs, especially for young families. The majority now offer rear half-doors on both sides, easing access to the rear seat. The rear seat is usually cramped, however, and is best used by younger, more limber passengers or for stowing gear. Extended-cab pickups typically offer less cargo and towing capacity than an identically equipped standard-cab counterpart, but the difference is small—typically just a few hundred pounds.

Then there are the true four-door pickups, often called crew cabs. Four-doors serve family, work, and travel needs better than any other cab configuration, which is why they are the most popular and best-selling model of pickups on the road, according to manufacturers' 2006 sales figures. Like extended-cab models, four-door models typically fall only a few hundred pounds shy of the cargo- and load-carrying capabilities offered by their regular-cab counterparts.

2007 Toyota Tundra pickup truck with a regular cab.

2007 Ford F-150 with an extended cab.

2007 GMC Sierra pickup with a four-door crew cab. (GMC/GENERAL MOTORS)

If you plan to haul a boat that has a trailered weight north of 6,000 pounds—such as a cabin cruiser—a four-door pickup with dual-rear wheels is far and away the most stable and comfortable pickup choice. The extra-wide rear footprint or *track* offered by a "dually" style pickup greatly improves towing stability.

The drawback of a dually style pickup is that it takes a lot more room to turn around, which can be a hassle in the close quarters of parking lots and smaller boat ramps. These trucks also tend to be less fuel-efficient and, because of the extra weight of their heavy-duty rear axle and suspension, tend to be rougher riding than their single-wheel counterparts.

If the boat you plan to tow weighs close to the towing limit of the truck model you're thinking about, you'll probably be happier with the longest wheelbase offered in that model. A longer wheelbase will be more stable when towing a trailer.

Model Recommendations

There are some fine half-ton, full-size pickup choices for towing boat trailers with surge-type brakes of 5,000 pounds or less. These include the F-150 Super Crew, the Chevy Silverado/GMC Sierra Crew Cab, the Dodge Ram Quad Cab, 2007 Toyota Tundra, and the Nissan Titan, all in either 2WD or 4WD configurations. When properly equipped, the three-quarter-ton (2500 series) models from Dodge, Ford, and GM also make excellent tow vehicles for trailers exceeding 5,000 pounds.

Let me point out that while I've noted the 2007 Toyota Tundra as a good choice for a tow vehicle, the previous year models of this pickup are not. That's because the owner's manual of previous versions clearly stated: "Do not exceed 45 mph or the posted trailer towing speed limit, whichever is lower" and "If towing a trailer and cargo weighing over 2000 pounds, it is necessary to use a sway control device with sufficient capacity."

In fact, such caveats should eliminate any vehicle from your list of boat towing candidates. Toyota has changed the 2007 Tundra owner's manual to reflect the all-new model's greater towing abilities, which no longer carries such stringent towing limitations.

For towing larger boats (i.e., tow packages that weigh more than 6,000 pounds), you might look toward the heavier-duty (three-quarter and one-ton) GMs, Dodges, and Fords, including duallys. Again, managing weight is what safe towing is all about, and nothing handles a trailer better than a pickup with a stout suspension and/or dual rear wheels.

2007 Chevrolet Silverado crew cab dually. (CHEVROLET/ GENERAL MOTORS)

SUVs and CUVs

When it comes to sport utility vehicles, name a brand and they probably have an SUV that can tow a boat. Even the smaller, more fuel-efficient SUVs such as the Ford Escape, Toyota Highlander, Jeep Liberty, and Honda Pilot can tow at least 3,500 pounds.

But mid- and full-size SUVs, such as the GMC Envoy, Yukon XL, Toyota 4Runner, Chevy Tahoe, and Ford Explorer, make better boat towing vehicles, simply because their size and weight make them more stable with a trailer in tow. They also provide a lot more interior passenger and storage space, which becomes a valued commodity when family and friends join the fun.

The Jeep Liberty is a small SUV, but it can still tow a family runabout.

SUVs have gained tremendous popularity over the last decade; they're a better fit for the boatowning family than a four-door pickup. An SUV will often fit in the garage while a full-size pickup doesn't clear the garage door. SUVs also have smaller turning radii and provide more secure cargo room.

Crossover SUVs, or CUVs, are a faster growing choice among new vehicle buyers. They are built on a unibody chassis, like cars, and they deliver a car-like ride, but they have the interior room of a conventional SUV. Models such as the Saturn Outlook, GMC Acadia, and Buick Enclave have 4,000-pound-plus tow ratings. Many now include automatic trailer sway control, too.

The drawback of a unibody design for boatowners is that any looseness between the hitch drawbar and the receiver will result in an annoying booming sound inside the vehicle when the boat is in tow, making you think the trailer has

The Chevy Tahoe is a large SUV with substantial towing capabilities. (CHEVROLET/GENERAL MOTORS)

come loose from the hitch ball. This phenomenon is worse on some CUVs than others, and there is no correlation with the price of the vehicle. The sound of the clanking hitch reverberates through the passenger compartment of a Mercedes just as annoyingly loud as it does inside a Kia.

This sound is caused by the way the hitch is attached to the body and how much or how little sound-deadening material the vehicle manufacturer has used to isolate the hitch noises from the passenger compartment. Unlike a hitch mounted to a frame that is isolated from the body, when the drawbar rattles against the square tube of a hitch mounted on a unibody chassis, that sound is sent into and magnified by the unibody, much like a tap on a drum.

My suggestion is to take a test drive with a boat in tow, paying careful attention not only to the power and handling of the vehicle but to the sounds it makes while towing. There are several aftermarket hitch accessories, such as the Quietride ball mount by Softride, Inc., designed to eliminate hitch rattle, however, so if you do end up with a noisy rig, you can quickly minimize the problem.

Model Recommendations

There are a hundred or more SUVs on the market, along with at least forty CUVs. Making a buying decision is tough. Good choices within the midsize SUV class include the Jeep Grand Cherokee/Commander, Dodge Durango, Ford Explorer, Nissan Pathfinder, Chevy TrailBlazer/GMC Envoy, Mitsubishi Endeavor, and Saab 9-7. Most are limited to 5,000 pounds or less weight-carrying tow capacity.

2007 Saturn Outlook is a CUV with decent towing capacity. (SATURN/GENERAL MOTORS)

Full-size CUVs that work well as tow vehicles for trailers up to 4,500 pounds include the Saturn Outlook, GMC Acadia and Buick Enclave. Full-size SUVs that handle boats well include the GMC Yukon/Yukon XL, the Chevrolet Tahoe/Suburban, the Ford Expedition, Chrysler Aspen, Toyota Land Cruiser, and Nissan Armada.

Gas or Diesel Engine?

This is an obvious and commonly asked question among boaters shopping for a new tow vehicle. Making a good engine choice has become more important than ever given the increasing fuel prices, and there is no pat answer. The choice depends in large part on your personal tastes and driving habits, the size of the boat your towing, and the conditions under which you'll use the vehicle.

In years past, diesels were noisy, smelly engines that were dogs when it came to accelerating onto a busy highway or passing slower-moving traffic. But recent advances in diesel technology have changed the way diesels perform. New diesels are far cleaner than their predecessors and possess better acceleration and pulling power than their strongest gasoline rivals. The turbocharged diesels found in trucks from Dodge, Ford, and GM are technological marvels, ideal for towing heavy loads in a sporty manner.

All three manufacturers have raised the performance of their engines in the past few years while reducing noise both inside and outside the cab. Computer-controlled turbos and four-, five-, and six-speed automatic transmissions allow them to accelerate quickly up on-ramps, making merging into flowing traffic and passing as easy as if you were driving a souped-up, big-block, gasoline V-8.

Diesel engines, like the GM Duramax, offer greater durability and torque than gasoline engines. (GM)

In fact, the new turbo-diesels—be they four-, six-, eight-, or ten-cylinders—are the kings of towing and hauling capacity within their respective engine groups, beating their gasoline counterparts in both engine longevity and fuel economy.

Such diesels have stump-pulling, low-rpm torque, which is what gets a load moving, along with fuel economy numbers better than their gasoline counterparts—especially with a boat in tow. It's not unusual to see 15 to 25 percent better highway fuel economy from diesels than gas engines, against which they compete. Those percentages usually—but not always—increase when towing a boat trailer, because a diesel generates a lot of low rpm pulling power; whereas, a gas engine needs to be wound up a little more to get the same performance. More throttle means more fuel used.

The drawback of diesel engines is that they usually require a lot of road miles to justify their higher initial cost. For instance, the typical diesel option in a full-size pickup will add about $6,500 to the base price of the truck, along with another $1,500–1,800 for an automatic, which is the transmission of choice among those who do a lot of city driving and towing.

Added to that, the price of diesel fuel in some areas is higher than that of regular unleaded, so the savings from enhanced fuel economy aren't quite as high as the Environmental Protection Agency (EPA) mileage figures might suggest.

Gasoline engines, like the GM Vortec, cost far less than diesels and offer better fuel economy when not towing a heavy load. (GM)

You also have to consider that diesels cost more to maintain in the short term. They require strict adherence to oil and filter changes every 2,500 to 3,500 miles, and their oil pans hold several more quarts of oil than a comparable gas engine. Air and fuel filters must also be checked and replaced more often than those in a gas engine.

The upside is that a well-maintained diesel will outlive a gas engine by a number of years and maybe more than 100,000 miles before a rebuild is required. And diesels don't require plug wires, spark plugs, ignition coils, and a number of other electrical components that require periodic replacement in a gas engine. So, over the long haul, so to speak, a diesel can be a good investment if you plan on keeping the tow vehicle around for 8 to 10 years and do a lot of towing/driving in the interim.

If these arguments don't sell you on diesel power, go with the largest gas engine offered in your vehicle model of choice. This is especially true in the compact and mid-size SUVs, pickups, and CUVs. A four-cylinder delivers good fuel economy, but it loses its appeal as soon as a boat is put on the hitch. You'll find that the smaller displacement engine has to be worked very hard with the extra load, and your fuel economy may well be worse than it would be with an I-5, V-6, or V-8 under the hood.

The same is true of most six-cylinder engines. Straight- and V-6 engines are strong performers in non-towing conditions, but when placed in full-size vehicles, they lack torque when it comes to towing. That's where a V-8 shines, making trailering easier and, in a way, safer. Today's V-8s are more powerful than ever before and provide gas mileage in the high teens to low twenties when used in non-towing situations on the open road. Put a trailer in tow, and those same vehicles will see fuel economy numbers in the low to mid double digits.

If several V-8s are optional, I prefer to get the biggest one offered. There's never been a time towing when I wished the engine were smaller. If your boat and trailer package weighs 8,000 pounds, get an engine of at least 300 horsepower—and diesel.

If you are buying a tow vehicle for lighter towing duties—say, for towing a boat/trailer rig weighing less than 5,000 pounds, a dozen or so times during the summer—a good choice would be a midsize (4.8- to 5.7-liter) V-8 engine with the best EPA rating.

Consider a five- or six-cylinder engine only if the boat/trailer combo you're towing weighs less than 4,000 pounds. The smaller engines just don't have the power for towing. And if you're looking at a compact pickup, SUV, or CUV to tow a smaller boat, it really doesn't pay to stick with the four-cylinder engine of the base model if you can get a six instead—unless that four-cylinder is a diesel!

Manual or Automatic Transmission?

Here's another controversial question, although it is far less of an issue now than it was a decade ago. Most trailer boaters consider an automatic as the only way to go, and automatics may be the only option in a few years. The new technology in automatics matches them perfectly to the engine and tow vehicle.

They shift precisely when needed, and they do so without undue strain or stress on the tow vehicle or the trailer in tow behind.

Newer automatics also provide low enough ratios in first gear to provide excellent grunt for pulling a loaded trailer smoothly up a steep boat ramp. Better still, some state-of-the-art automatics are computer-controlled, allowing *grade braking* and *tow/haul* modes, which cause the transmission to shift down, delay shifting, or hold a lower gear in response to how you are accelerating or braking at any given moment. Such smart automatics make towing a loaded trailer a lot easier on both the vehicle and the driver.

A few owners of larger boats say they would never drive anything but a manual transmission. But that's old-school thinking, and if those boatowners were to drive a tow vehicle with a state-of-the-art, five- or six-speed automatic transmission, they would change that tune. What manual-transmission aficionados seem to forget is that the clutch is a serious weak point, and trying to master the simultaneous use of gas, brake, and clutch pedals at a boat ramp is more than the novice boater needs to deal with. Slipping a clutch to get the tow vehicle moving is hard on the clutch. Do that a couple of times, and you can almost bet a costly clutch replacement is in the works.

A 4WD system allows the driver to choose when to engage and disengage the front wheels.

If in doubt, do what 95 percent of today's pickup and SUV buyers do—get the automatic. If that hasn't sold you, know this: tow vehicles with automatics generally have greater tow ratings than models with manual transmissions.

Two-, Four-, or All-Wheel Drive?

Traction at a boat ramp is a key issue when choosing your tow vehicle. Some concrete ramps are very slick from heavy use, algae, silt, or other deposits. Other ramps may be nothing more than gravel or mud.

A slick or soft ramp surface can make getting your boat out of the water tricky. When your tow vehicle's tires start spinning, forward momentum decreases or stops, and a lot of unneeded wear on the spinning tire or tires begins. Boaters who plan on spending a lot of time enjoying the water should seriously consider choosing a vehicle that has four-wheel drive (4WD) or all-wheel drive (AWD).

The basic difference between the two is that 4WD vehicles have a control that allows the driver to select when the vehicle is applying traction to both the front and rear axles. Most AWD vehicles handle that control through the vehicle's onboard computer, without any driver intervention or knowledge. Both systems work equally well around a boat ramp.

Some 4WD systems also allow the driver to choose either high-range or low-range transmission gearing modes. Think of high-range as the normal transmission gearing and low-range as one in which the engine has to rev higher to achieve the same ground speed. Low-range 4WD mode makes it easier for the tow vehicle to get a heavy load moving without straining the engine.

A 4WD or AWD option usually adds several thousand dollars to the price of a vehicle and typically reduces highway fuel economy by 1 or 2 miles per gallon (mpg). However, the added traction they provide is well worth the trade-offs.

MUST-HAVE OPTIONS

The mistake a lot of new vehicle buyers make isn't buying the wrong tow vehicle, but rather buying the right tow vehicle with the wrong options. It's easy to walk around a dealer's lot and see a vehicle that seems just perfect, but it may be missing options that would make it more suitable for towing your boat.

Tow Package

If the vehicle dealer is on the ball, the pickup, CUV, or SUV you are eyeing probably has the factory tow package. Most tow packages include a heavy-duty cooling system with a heavy-duty radiator, oil cooler, and transmission oil cooler to protect the engine and transmission from overheating under the constant load of a trailer (Chapter 8). These upgrades can be added after the fact using either original equipment manufacturers' (OEM) or aftermarket components, but doing so will cost you two to three times more in parts and labor as the option would cost from the factory.

Some towing packages also include a heavy-duty alternator, heavy-duty battery, and a special wiring harness to connect the trailer's lights and electric brakes. The heavy-duty, higher-output alternator and battery system handles the additional loads required by the trailer lights (and possibly other accessories, such as an electric winch or tongue jack). Most new tow vehicle packages come with a seven-pin round plug socket, while many boat trailers come with four- or five-pin connectors, so you may have to buy a flat-four-(or five-) to-round-seven pin adapter. (The extra pins in a seven-pin connector are mainly used to power various accessories on recreational vehicles, and rarely come into play on boat trailers.) These adapters are available at just about any auto parts store or any retailer that carries such towing products as hitches and tow balls. The adapter is sometimes included as part of a new vehicle's towing package.

A round seven-to-flat-five wiring adapter. The round part mates with the tow vehicle's wiring harness, while the flat part connects to the trailer's plug.

(CEQUENT GROUP)

The typical towing package also includes a receiver hitch matched to the vehicle and its towing capabilities. Almost invariably on full-size pickups and SUVs, the factory hitch will be a Class III (5,000-pound weight-carrying capacity) or a Class IV (7,500-pound weight-carrying capacity) model. Rarely will the hitch be a heavy-duty Class V, which has a weight-carrying capacity of up to 12,000 pounds. CUVs typically have a Class II (3,500-pound capacity) or Class III hitch. (See Chapter 3 for more information on hitch classes.)

Other towing package components may include beefed-up shocks and springs and heavy-duty brakes with larger drums and heavy-duty linings.

Differential Gear Ratios

Remembering to order the tow package option is easy. It's the other important towing-related options that often get bypassed by those new to towing a boat. A prime example is the differential gear ratio, which describes the number of times the driveshaft turns for each rotation of the wheel. (Optional axle ratios are only available on RWD and 4WD trucks. They are not offered on FWD vehicles, but FWD is generally only available on cars that are not appropriate for towing boats in any case.)

For example, a typical V-8 pickup or SUV comes with an axle ratio between 3.31:1 and 3.55:1. This means that for every 3.3 or 3.5 turns of the driveshaft, the rear wheels make one rotation. Assuming that two vehicles have the same size tires, the engine in the one with the numerically higher axle ratio (e.g., 3.31:1 as opposed to 3.55:1) will run at a lower rpm at any given highway speed, and that means better highway fuel economy. A factory's standard gearing delivers what the engineers feel is the best compromise between fuel economy and overall performance when the pickup is driven without a tow. But it isn't necessarily the best gear ratio for boat towing applications.

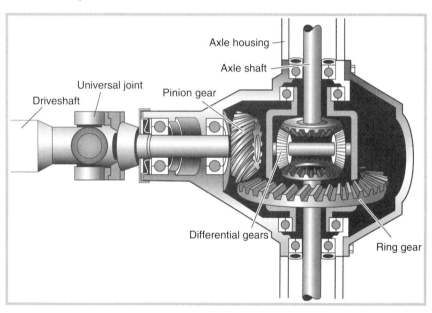

The axle gear ratio—the number of times the driveshaft turns for each turn of the wheels—affects towing capabilities, acceleration, and fuel economy. (TRAILER BOATS)

The highway gearing causes the engine to lug or strain under the added load of a trailer, which in turn causes you to get deeper into the throttle to maintain cruising speeds. More throttle means more fuel used and more stress on the drivetrain. That is precisely why vehicle manufacturers offer optional axle ratios.

To maximize your new vehicle's towing performance, order a tow vehicle with an axle gear ratio of at least 3.73:1. Even better is 3.92:1 or 4.10:1. A numerically higher axle gear ratio will greatly improve acceleration, cruising, and engine braking performance when you have a trailer in tow.

Don't fret about how such gearing might affect your fuel economy. Automotive engineers say the numerically higher gear ratio will raise engine speed a couple of hundred rpm on the open highway, but doing so will reduce fuel economy only slightly in non-towing modes. In fact, their tests show that city fuel economy will not change noticeably. And when there's a trailer in tow, your fuel

FUEL ECONOMY AND TOWING ABILITY

Hang around a car dealership for any length of time and you will hear buyers automatically asking about a potential tow vehicle's fuel economy. That's one of the main reasons pickup and SUV buyers, who make up half of today's car market, choose smaller V-8s rather than more powerful engines, even though the EPA fuel numbers are sometimes remarkably similar.

After the purchase, however, drivers come to realize that in the real world, a bigger engine is not always bad. Put a load in a pickup or SUV, or hitch up a boat trailer, and it's possible that the smaller engine will get poorer fuel economy because it has to work harder.

Similarly, a buyer might think that the standard or base axle ratio, which is typically 3.42:1 or 3.55:1, will give better fuel economy than a 3.73:1 or 3.92:1 ratio, but such thinking may be short-sighted. Manufacturers offer optional axle ratios for one reason: to improve a vehicle's towing performance.

A lower (numerically higher) gear ratio provides more low-speed wheel torque, which makes it easier to get the vehicle moving when pulling a trailer or carrying a load of passengers and cargo. Lower gears also improve acceleration up to about 60 mph. (Passing performance and speeds above 60 mph depend on horsepower not axle ratio.)

The next time you buy a new tow vehicle, make sure you scan the options list closely and put a checkmark next to 3.73:1, 3.92:1, or 4.10:1 optional axle ratio. You'll be happy with the decision.

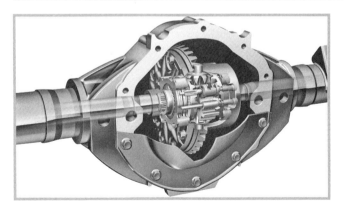

A locking differential improves traction on slippery boat ramps. (GM)

economy may actually be better than it would be with a highway gear ratio because the engine isn't pushed as hard to maintain a given speed.

Limited-Slip and Locking Differentials

Boaters should also consider ordering the factory *limited-slip* differential, which generally adds $250 to $400 to the vehicle purchase price. When one wheel begins to slip, the clutches or gears inside the limited-slip differential transfer some of the drivetrain power to the wheel with better traction. The actual names of these units vary from manufacturer to manufacturer, but in essence a limited-slip differential provides considerably more traction when ramp or road conditions are slippery.

Even better than a limited-slip differential is a *locking* differential, or *locker*. Whether actuated manually by a switch on the dash or console or automatically, a locker literally locks both wheels on the same axle together to function as one, thus marshaling the maximum traction available from your vehicle.

If you already own a tow vehicle and want to improve its traction on slick or unimproved boat ramps, an ARB Air Locker installation is a great choice. An Air Locker will maximize boat ramp traction while keeping handling and tire wear unaffected. It is, at the time of this writing, the only air-activated traction improver of its type on the market. If you have a good working knowledge of differentials, you can install the Air Locker yourself. Otherwise, have the installation done by a shop knowledgeable in axles and differentials.

ARB Air Lockers are air-actuated devices that are installed inside the rear axle as part of the gear set. When traction deteriorates, you push a button on the dash, which instantly opens a pressurized-air line that forces the Air Locker to engage the drive wheels on both sides. This action provides the maximum traction available and is great on slippery or unimproved boat ramps. The ARB Air Locker engages and disengages in less than a tenth of a second.

The ARB Air Locker is an aftermarket locking differential kit that you can add to your vehicle if it isn't equipped with a factory unit. (ARB USA)

The difference between an ARB Air Locker and a conventional locking differential is that the driver exercises absolute control over the Air Locker. Conventional lockers lock and unlock automatically when they sense a threshold difference in rotation between the wheels on the drive axle.

An added benefit of an air-actuated locker is that it gives you an onboard air supply with which to keep tow vehicle and trailer tires inflated—not to mention the air mattresses and other inflatable items commonly found on a boating outing.

An electrically operated locker is now available as an option on some models of GM pickups and SUVs and will probably become an option on other brands. It operates similarly to the ARB Air Locker except that when the vehicle operator pushes the dash-mounted switch, an electric solenoid in the axle housing, rather than air pressure, does the locking work. An ARB Air Locker can cost upward of $1,000 for the unit and its installation, while a factory-installed electric locking differential runs closer to $400.

Other Options

When you get ready to buy your new tow vehicle, check out various tire and wheel options and see how they rate for towing compared with the stock ones. In most instances, the weight of a boat/trailer combination is well within the weight limitations of optional tires and wheels. But in some cases the 20- to 22-inch tire/wheel options reduce the vehicles's tow ratings. To be sure, check the tire rating located on the sidewall, or look at the tire's specifications, which the vehicle dealer should have on hand. If the vehicle's rear gross axle weight rating

(RGAWR) combined with the tongue weight of the loaded trailer is less than double the maximum load-carrying limit of the tire (since the load is carried by both rear tires), you're fine. (If the vehicle is a dually, divide by four instead of two, since there are four tires on the rear axle.) Pay particular attention to this if the optional wheels or tires are a different size from the standard equipment. Before changing size, consult the owner's manual or ask the dealer.

Often the optional tire and wheel package is well-suited to towing a boat trailer and will give your vehicle a nicer look. But don't buy the option if you want to match the boat trailer's tires and wheels to those of the tow vehicle, because the automaker's optional wheels may be difficult or impossible to match for your trailer. A better plan is to buy the two vehicles with the less expensive standard-equipment wheels, then buy matching wheels and tires for the tow vehicle and the trailer at the same time from a tire store or wheel accessories dealer.

Extended side-view mirrors—also called towing mirrors—sometimes come as part of the tow package. If not, you can order them as an option. Check your state laws for possible mirror requirements for towing (see Appendix B). Make sure your tow vehicle has mirrors that allow you to see beyond the trailer, which aids not only on the open road but also when maneuvering in and around boat ramps and parking lots. A good set of towing mirrors should extend far enough from the cab to give the driver a clear view of the boat trailer's wheels, and it's even better if you can see the sides of the trailer all the way to the end.

Some optional towing mirrors are adjustable in length and can be extended, angled, or retracted to work in many different towing situations. Others have a

Custom matching wheels and tires on the tow vehicle and trailer are a nice touch. Make sure they're the same size as the stock items, and that the tires can handle the load. (TRAILER BOATS)

fixed length. Get electric adjustable mirrors if they are available. Any number of aftermarket towing mirrors are available to fit just about every vehicle on the road.

It also pays to mount a wide-angle convex spot mirror inside the standard mirror. This little mirror has a self-adhesive back so you can attach it directly to the factory or aftermarket mirror. The resultant view helps not only when backing down a boat ramp or positioning the boat trailer back home, but also in seeing any vehicles in the blind spots to each side of the tow vehicle.

Blind spots are the main cause of towing accidents involving other vehicles on the open road. One is to the driver's left, just behind the driver's door and ahead of the rear bumper; the other is over the driver's right shoulder, between the passenger's door and the rear bumper and extending several vehicle widths.

Telescoping side-view mirrors allow you to see around a wide boat and trailer but retract for a slimmer profile when you're not towing. A convex auxiliary mirror, like the one on the bottom of this unit, helps you see other vehicles that might be lurking in your blind spot on the highway. (FORD MOTOR COMPANY)

TEST-DRIVES

Finally, take a test-drive. There's no better way to see if a vehicle fits your needs than to get behind the wheel and go for a ride. Don't just drive around the block—actually drive it. After all, you're about to make a significant investment, and you want it to be the right choice.

Ask the salesman if it's OK to go hook up that boat and trailer. Note how the vehicle responds under various circumstances; for example:

- Pay close attention to how the brakes and throttle pedal respond to driver input.
- Pay attention to overall visibility from the driver's seat.
- Are the controls easy to reach?
- Check out how the steering feels and the wheel's turning radius.
- Take it out on the freeway and also drive it around town for a few minutes. How does it feel towing the boat?
- Take a back road so you can drive over a few potholes and gravel sections.
- How much road noise can you feel and hear?
- Are the seats comfortable?
- How is visibility to the rear and sides?
- Sit in the back seat for a short time while a friend drives. Is it comfortable?

When you have a good feel for the truck, fill the fuel tank and thank the salesman. If you are deciding between different vehicles, go to your next candidate and repeat the process. If the dealer has the same pickup in stock with a different engine or gear ratio, take it out so you have a comparison. Such a test-drive regimen takes time, but it pays big dividends in the long run.

Test-drive the tow vehicle in a variety of conditions—including in traffic—with your boat and trailer in tow.

Matching Your Boat/Trailer to a Tow Vehicle

Towing is easier, safer, and more pleasant when you're driving a tow vehicle that's well-matched to your boat and trailer. Below are some guidelines to help you choose the right vehicle:

- Assuming your boat trailer has surge brakes, select a tow vehicle that has a weight-carrying capacity 10 to 25 percent greater than the weight of the loaded boat and trailer
- Do not select a vehicle according to its weight-distributing tow rating if your trailer has a surge braking system unless you plan on adding an electric hydraulic brake system to your boat trailer.
- Don't rely on the salesman's word or the advertising literature regarding tow ratings. Use the tow ratings specified in the owner's manual to make your determinations.
- An automatic transmission is better than a manual when towing boats.
- Numerically higher axle gear ratios, such as 3.73:1 or even 4.10:1 are best for towing.
- When available, always select the limited-slip or locking differential option.
- Always choose the optional tow package, regardless of the vehicle.
- Retractable towing mirrors are a good tow vehicle option.
- 4WD and AWD are beneficial on slick ramps.
- Longer-wheelbase vehicles make better tow vehicles than those with short wheelbases.

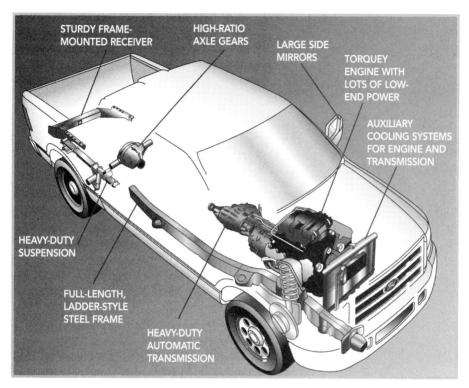

STURDY FRAME-
MOUNTED RECEIVER

HIGH-RATIO
AXLE GEARS

LARGE SIDE
MIRRORS

TORQUEY
ENGINE WITH
LOTS OF LOW-
END POWER

AUXILIARY
COOLING SYSTEMS
FOR ENGINE AND
TRANSMISSION

HEAVY-DUTY
SUSPENSION

FULL-LENGTH,
LADDER-STYLE
STEEL FRAME

HEAVY-DUTY
AUTOMATIC
TRANSMISSION

Characteristics of a good tow vehicle. (FORD MOTOR COMPANY)

- Diesels are a good cost-reducing choice for towing heavier loads over longer distances.
- Four-door pickups are more convenient for families than two-door and extended-cab models.
- Large SUVs and crossover SUVs (called CUVs) make good tow vehicles for families.
- Forget compact SUVs, CUVs, cars, or minivans for towing unless the boat and trailer are very light.

3

Trailer Hitches

Alas, we're not finished with the numbers. Like the vehicles they are attached to, hitches have their own limits or ratings, and exceeding those limits can result in some very unpleasant towing situations. As boaters committed to doing things right and safely, let's plow on.

HITCH RATINGS

Automotive trailer hitches come in four basic classifications—Classes I, II, III, and IV—based on specifications and test criteria set forth by the Society of Automotive Engineers International (SAE) in Standard J684. A few hitch manufacturers have also begun to use a Class V designation to indicate a super-heavy-duty, frame-mounted hitch designed for towing trailers that weigh up to 15,000 pounds. Although SAE has yet to make this classification official, it exists as a de facto standard.

These classes are shown in the table below.

All of the weight ratings mentioned above are for the weight-carrying capacity of the hitch assembly (i.e., dead weight), not the weight-distributing rating, which requires additional hardware to be installed on the hitch/trailer. There

Table 3.1	CAPACITY BY TOWING HITCH CLASSIFICATIONS (in pounds)				
	Class I	Class II	Class III	Class IV	Class V (not an official SAE class)
Maximum Weight-Carrying Capacity (gross trailer weight)	2,000	3,500	5,000	10,000	12,000–15,000
Maximum Tongue Weight (TW)	200	350	500	1,000	1,500

are two types of hitch-weight ratings: gross trailer weight (GTW), which is the weight of the loaded trailer, and tongue weight (TW). We'll cover more on GTW in Chapter 4; for now, let's look at TW.

Tongue Weight

Tongue weight is the amount of weight the trailer places on the hitch ball. Too little weight on the tongue can cause the trailer to sway from side-to-side when being towed; too much weight can cause the front of the tow vehicle to rise, possibly reducing steering control and braking efficiency.

While vehicle manufacturers generally specify that travel or cargo trailer tongue weight should be between 10 and 15 percent of the loaded trailer weight, these specifications don't apply to boat trailers. The reason is that boat trailer manufacturers distribute weight differently over the axles than most travel and cargo trailers. Consequently, boat trailer manufacturers typically specify that TW should be between 5 and 10 percent of the GTW.

But while attending to TW, it's important not to lose sight of the tow vehicle's tow rating (Chapter 2) or the maximum weight-carrying capacity of the hitch. In other words, both the gross trailer weight rating (GTWR) and the TW limits must be observed—not one or the other.

Light-Duty Hitches

Class I

The most basic hitch, and commonly found on small cars, minivans, and compact SUVs, is the Class I category. Class I hitches, which are designed to handle a GTW up to 2,000 pounds and a TW up to 200 pounds, comprise three basic types:

- Receiver hitch: Uses a $1\frac{1}{4}"$ receiver tube. The towing ball is attached to a drawbar that slips into the receiver and is held in place with a locking pin.
- Non-receiver hitch: Mounts to the vehicle's frame or unibody chassis. The towing ball is attached directly to a flange or platform on the hitch itself.
- Towing ball: Fastens directly to the vehicle's rear bumper.

It is important to know that the tow ratings of many vehicles equipped with factory-supplied Class I hitches are lower than the Class I hitch requirements. In some cases, the ratings are as low as 1,000 pounds (or even less) for the GTW, and 100 pounds or less for the TW. Although the Class I hitch must meet the SAE standards for the class, other aspects of the vehicle itself may not have been engineered to handle those loads, so the vehicle manufacturers will impose lower ratings accordingly.

One common reason for such low towing limits is lightweight hitch mounts, in which the hitch is bolted to the floor pan of a unibody vehicle with little (if any) reinforcement to the sheet metal at the mounting points. Bumper-mounted hitches are also frequently under-engineered. Today's vehicle bumpers are generally made of a light alloy or aluminum. Some are steel, but few have sufficient strength to handle anything but the lightest loads. Aluminum ones are also

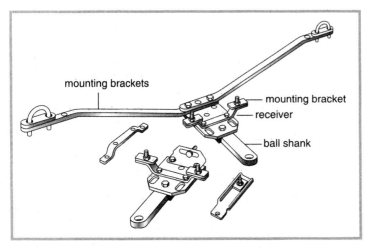

mounting brackets

mounting bracket

receiver

ball shank

A Class I hitch, rated for a GTW up to 2,000 pounds and a TW up to 200 pounds. (TRAILER BOATS)

problematic, because a galvanic reaction can occur between the bumper alloy and the steel hitch, which can lead to corrosion and eventual failure of the components.

Yet another problem with bumper-mounted hitches is that they interfere with the bumper's energy-absorbing system, which is designed to soften low-speed impacts, such as parking-lot incidents. If the hitch attaches to both the bumper and the floor pan, then the energy-absorbing function is totally disabled. On the other hand, if the hitch ball is attached only to the bumper, then the stress of towing a trailer can, over time, damage the shock-absorbing units.

Step-bumper hitches found on some smaller trucks don't always have tow ratings, and some are strictly for decorative purposes. Even though a step bumper may have a hole drilled through it for a hitch ball, the bumper itself may not be strong enough to handle the load placed on it by a bouncing boat trailer.

Thus before you drop a boat trailer on a step bumper's hitch ball, be sure the bumper is properly constructed for towing and that it has a tow rating stamped into the metal. If there's no rating, don't use that vehicle to tow anything until it is properly equipped. Some automotive original equipment manufacturers (OEM), as well as many aftermarket manufacturers, offer easy-to-install step bumpers with respectable tow ratings.

Class II

Class II hitches are also considered light duty and use the small $1\frac{1}{4}$" receiver tube. These hitches are commonly found on compact pickups, CUVs, and SUVs as a factory-installed option. The difference is they typically mount directly to the vehicle at four points: on the chassis, if the vehicle is so equipped, or to reinforced points on the floor pan of a unibody vehicle. The stronger mounting locations increase the GTW to 3,500 pounds and a maximum trailer TW of 350 pounds. As always, the vehicle itself may have a lower tow rating than the hitch.

A Class II hitch, rated for a GTW up to 3,500 pounds and a TW up to 350 pounds. (TRAILER BOATS)

Class I and II hitches work well for small aluminum or fiberglass boats up to about 17 feet.

Hitches for Heavier Loads

Class III and Hybrid

When boat lengths get much beyond 17 feet, it's time for a step up in hitch selection. That's where the Class III hitch plays a big role.

These medium-duty hitches are quite popular on full-size pickups and mid-size/full-size SUVs. They use a 2-inch-square receiver tube and mount to the vehicle frame or unibody in at least six places—three along each side. This stronger design gives a Class III hitch a GTW of 5,000 pounds, with 500 pounds of TW. Such hitches are adequate for many boats up to about 24 feet.

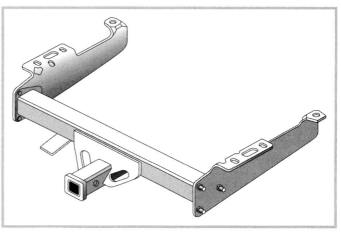

A Class III hitch, rated for a GTW up to 5,000 pounds and a TW up to 500 pounds. (TRAILER BOATS)

An even better choice is a hybrid version of the Class III, known as a Class III/IV. It too is also common on full-size pickups and SUVs. A hybrid has a GTW range of 6,000 to 9,000 pounds (depending on vehicle and hitch manufacturer/design) and TW ratings up to 1,000 pounds, which cover many types of fishing or family pleasure boats up to 26 feet.

Class IV

When you get to 28- to 30-foot cabin-style boats on tandem- and triple-axle trailers, you need a heavy-duty hitch. This is where the true Class IV hitch comes into play.

These large, heavy-gauge steel hitches are stouter in design and material than the hybrid Class III/IV models and are used on three-quarter- and one-ton pickups and SUVs designed for towing big trailers. They have a GTW of 10,000 pounds and a TW of 1,000 pounds. When available from the factory, they are usually part of a special heavy-duty towing package. More often, however, they are installed as an aftermarket accessory.

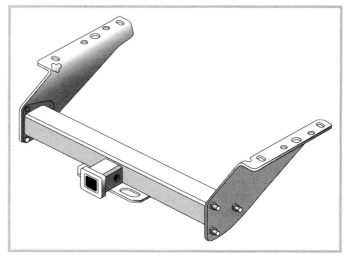

A Class IV hitch, rated for a GTW up to 10,000 pounds and a TW up to 1,000 pounds. (TRAILER BOATS)

Class V

Class V receiver hitches are available only as aftermarket add-ons because they aren't recognized by SAE Standard J684 as an official classification. These

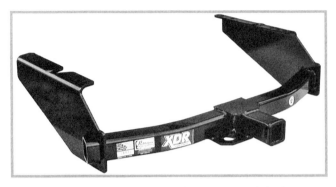

A Class V hitch, rated for a GTW up to 15,000 pounds and a TW up to 1,500 pounds.

(CEQUENT GROUP)

monster hitches, with a GTW of 15,000 pounds and TW rating of 1,500 pounds, are available from only a few sources.

The boats requiring a Class V hitch are typically big, overwide cruisers or offshore fishing boats that spend the majority of their time sitting in slips rather than on a trailer in the back yard. Very few first-time boaters will be taking on such a boat/trailer combination, and there are only a couple pickups on the market with the necessary towing abilities. But if the boat you want to tow is that big, rest assured there's a weight-carrying hitch to handle the task—if the truck can.

WEIGHT-DISTRIBUTING HITCHES AND SWAY-CONTROL DEVICES

We've spent lot of time talking about weight-carrying hitch capacities with little mention of weight-distributing hitches—for good reason. Weight-distributing hitches, as mentioned before, are not popularly used on trailers equipped with surge brakes, which includes the majority of boat trailers.

Weight-distributing hitches, also called load-equalizing hitches, use special bars to make a mechanical bridge between the trailer and tow vehicle, greatly increasing the vehicle's maximum trailer-towing limits.

A weight-distributing system consists of a frame-mounted receiver and spring bars (also called equalizing bars) that attach to a special ball-mount assembly

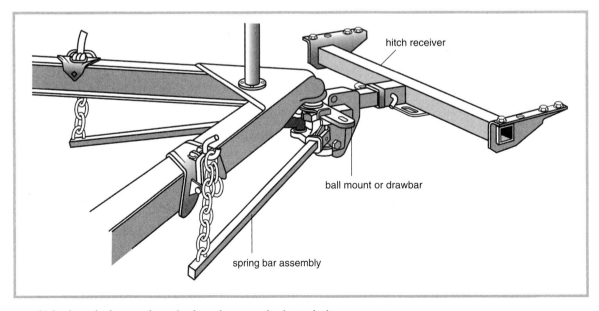

hitch receiver

ball mount or drawbar

spring bar assembly

A weight-distributing hitch may not be used with a trailer equipped with surge brakes. (TRAILER BOATS)

and to a trailer-tongue-mounted platform (see bottom illustration opposite). The bars have chains connected to brackets mounted on the trailer tongue. The length of the chains can be changed to adjust distribution of the TW.

These spring bars act like handles on a wheelbarrow. As the spring bars are raised, some of the TW is lifted off the tow vehicle's rear wheels and shifted forward to the front wheels and rearward to the trailer's axle(s). Unfortunately, this arrangement interferes with the operation of a trailer's surge braking system.

A boat trailer tongue must move freely forward and backward by as much as an inch for a surge brake system to function properly. When you step on the brakes in a tow vehicle, the trailer's momentum causes the coupler to press hard against the hitch ball. The coupler moves back a bit on the trailer's tongue on a sliding mount, depressing a hydraulic master cylinder inside the coupler. This

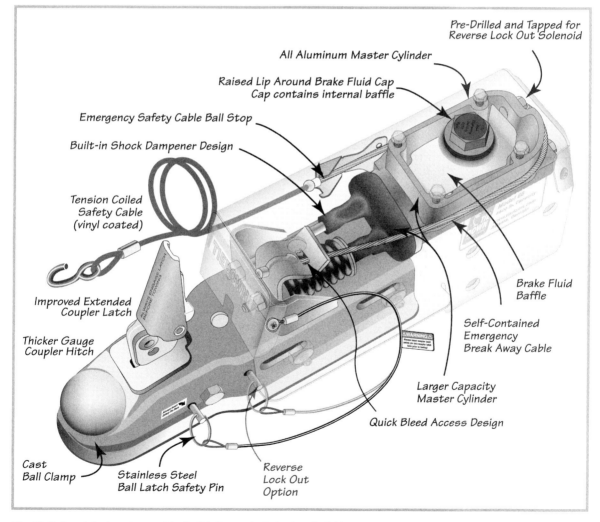

A boat trailer's surge brake system, contained within the coupler, is simple and reliable. (TIEDOWN ENGINEERING)

WEIGHT-DISTRIBUTING HITCH FOR SURGE BRAKE SYSTEMS

Using a weight-distributing hitch on a boat trailer equipped with surge brakes is generally not recommended by boat trailer manufacturers because such hitches can possibly cause binding on the coupler and interfere with the surge brake actuator. But there is one weight-distributing hitch designed specifically for boat trailers: the Equal-i-zer Hitch from Progress Manufacturing.

The Equal-i-zer Hitch is a unique weight-distributing hitch that's compatible with surge brakes. (PROGRESS MANUFACTURING)

On weight-distributing hitches, spring bars transfer a portion of the trailer's tongue weight from the hitch to the front of the tow vehicle and rear of the trailer. Progress states that the Equal-i-zer Hitch is unique among weight-distributing hitches because, instead of being attached in a fixed manner to the trailer, the spring bars slide in special brackets. This construction allows the trailer coupler to move fore-and-aft so the hydraulic brake cylinder inside the coupler can operate normally.

To install this hitch:

1. Clamp the mounting brackets for the sliding spring bars to the boat trailer. (Pole-tongue trailers require an adapter kit.)
2. Slide the hitch into the tow vehicle's weight-distributing Class IV or V receiver.
3. Position the spring bars in their brackets beneath the trailer.
4. Adjust the brackets so the distribution of the trailer weight results in the frames of the tow vehicle and trailer being parallel with the road—or with a very slight bow-down angle on the trailer.

Progress Manufacturing claims the hitch also has a built-in sway-control function.

activates the slave cylinders in the wheels, just as in a car's braking system.

The beauty of a surge braking system is that the mechanical pressure generated by the coupler pressing against the hitch ball is proportional to the braking of the tow vehicle (i.e., the harder you step on the brake, the harder the trailer brakes are applied). But with spring arms connecting the trailer to the hitch, the coupler loses some or all of its freedom of movement, and the braking system is impaired or disabled.

Some hitch sellers assert that weight-distributing hitches can be used on boat trailers if owners install a pole-tongue adapter kit, and then adjust the spring-bar chains to a very specific angle. Nevertheless, it's the boat trailer manufacturer who has the final say as to whether or not weight-distributing hitches are safe for that trailer application. Most will say "no."

That being the case, it's best to avoid the use of *any* weight-distributing hitches in which spring bars are anchored or fixed at either end and so preventing the free fore/aft movement of the surge brake trailer coupler.

Given the limited availability of boat trailers equipped with systems other than surge brakes, you may need to step up to a bigger tow vehicle if your boat/trailer package is over the weight-carrying limits of your existing tow vehicle.

If a new and bigger tow vehicle is out of the picture, here is a less costly alternative: the Equal-i-zer Hitch from Progress Manufacturing. This weight-distributing hitch is designed to allow the spring bars to slide enough for a boat trailer's surge brakes to function normally while also distributing the trailer load evenly across tow vehicle and trailer. See the accompanying sidebar for more information on this innovative hitch.

Sway-control devices are also recommended or required by many tow vehicle manufacturers for towing above certain weight limits. This device is a separate piece of hardware that is attached between the trailer tongue and the hitch to prevent or inhibit the trailer from swaying side-to-side. Like weight-distributing hitches, sway-control devices will interfere with the function of surge brakes and are not recommended by trailer and trailer component manufacturers.

If your towing vehicle requires the use of a weight-distributing hitch and/or a sway-control device to haul the weight of your boat and trailer, the solution to the problem is to use a trailer with electric or electric/hydraulic brakes. Both types of brakes are compatible with weight-distributing hitches and sway-control devices, and can be found as either optional or standard equipment on many new double- and triple-axle trailers. (It is also important to know surge-type trailer brakes do not work while backing downhill—or down a slick boat ramp. They only work when there is compression between the coupler and the tow ball.)

OTHER HITCH HARDWARE

Except for some Class I hitches, all hitches for boat trailers are receiver types. The receiver is a square-sectioned tube, made to accept a similarly shaped drawbar, to which the hitch ball is attached.

Drawbars are available in a variety of configurations, with straight, dropped, or raised shanks to allow a match between the height of the receiver and the height of the trailer's coupler. Some dropped shanks may be inverted to serve as a raised shank if need be, and some have adjustable shanks that can be raised or lowered. Other drawbars allow multiple hitch balls to be mounted simultaneously, so a tow vehicle can tow trailers with a variety of coupler sizes.

SAE has defined hitch ball requirements for each of the four official classes of trailer hitch, based on the weight of the trailer and its cargo (the gross towed weight rating, GTWR). Although actual hitch ball capacities vary from manufacturer to manufacturer, they all must meet the minimums defined by the SAE and shown in the table on page 51. Note that the ball's capacity is keyed to its shank diameter, and that the nut holding the hitch ball to the hitch or drawbar must be tightened to a specific torque for each class. It's important to periodically check the nut's tightness and to inspect the ball and its shank for signs of stress cracking or excessive wear.

COMBO BARS FOR PICKUP CAMPERS

Many boaters tow boats behind pickup campers, which are pickup trucks with a slide-in camper in the bed. If the camper extends beyond the back of the bed, the trailer tongue may not reach the hitch, and there may be no clearance for the boat trailer to turn without hitting the camper.

Receiver-hitch extension kits, commonly called combo bars, solve both problems. Most hitch installation and recreational vehicle (RV) sales centers offer such kits, or they can fabricate an extension using a piece of 2 × 2 receiver stock.

One end of the combo bar slips into the pickup's receiver and the other is bent at an angle so it can be attached to the vehicle's bumper. The result is a receiver at the end of the camper that can accept a standard 2 × 2 drop-shank hitch.

Extending the hitch in this manner comes at a price, however. Because of the added leverage placed on the hitch mounting points, maximum TW should be reduced. Consult the manufacturer of the combo bar to find out by how much.

A variety of drawbars, including (left to right) drop-shank, straight, reversible (drop- or raised-shank), adjustable height, and multiple-ball versions.
(CEQUENT GROUP)

Manufacturers clearly identify every component of a towing package with its class and weight ratings. Balls, drawbars, and couplers have their class stamped directly into the steel, as well as the ball diameter on balls and couplers, as shown in the photos. Hitches typically have labels that identify classes.

Table 3.2	HITCH BALL SIZES, WEIGHT LIMITS, AND TORQUE SPECIFICATIONS			
Hitch Class	**Ball Size**	**Nut Torque (foot-pounds)**	**Shank Diameter**	**GTWR (in pounds)**
Class I	$1\frac{7}{8}$"	85	$\frac{3}{4}$"	2,000
			1"	3,500
Class II	2"	105	$\frac{3}{4}$"	3,500
			1"	6,000
			$1\frac{1}{4}$"	8,000
			$1\frac{3}{8}$"	10,000
Class III	2"	235	$\frac{3}{4}$"	3,500
			1"	6,000
			$1\frac{1}{4}$"	8,000
			$1\frac{3}{8}$"	10,000
Class IV	2"	300	$\frac{3}{4}$"	3,500
			1"	6,000
			$1\frac{1}{4}$"	8,000
			$1\frac{3}{8}$"	10,000
Class V	$2\frac{5}{16}$"	300	1"	6,000
			$1\frac{1}{4}$"	15,000

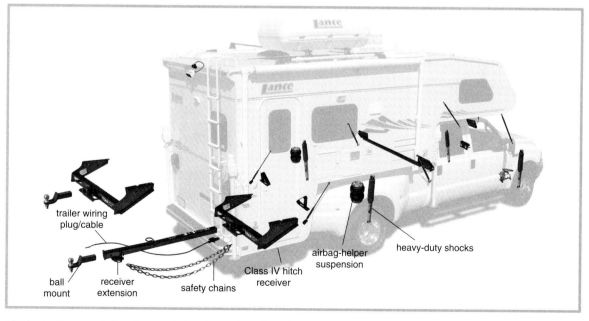

trailer wiring plug/cable

ball mount

receiver extension

safety chains

Class IV hitch receiver

airbag-helper suspension

heavy-duty shocks

A hitch extension or combo bar allows you to tow a boat trailer with a pickup camper by extending the hitch ball out past the camper. (LANCE CAMPER MANUFACTURING CORP.)

Hitches, hitch balls, drawbars, and trailer couplers are all clearly identified with their SAE class rating.

4

Choosing and Equipping Your Trailer

The bigger the boat, the bigger the tow trailer you need, and the bigger the trailer, the more expensive it becomes. With that increase in price comes more options, which complicate your choices but can also increase your enjoyment of boating. Advances in technology have introduced a lot of great products for both boats and trailers, and in this chapter, we'll take a look at the latter.

The most basic, inexpensive boat trailer has a painted steel frame, carpeted board bunks, a single axle, and no brakes. These are the trailers you see underneath the smallest aluminum and fiberglass fishing skiffs and duck hunters' jonboats. On small boats—those less than 17 feet long or so—a single axle is all that's needed. As boat size and weight increase, additional axles are added to make the load more manageable, and larger trailers require brakes as mandated state by state.

Years ago, manufacturers of trailerable boats often sold their boats without trailers. Good boat dealers usually had an assortment of trailers in inventory and would gladly recommend one to fit the boat and the buyer's budget. Most of the time that arrangement worked well. The dealer was well-versed not only in trailer brands but also in the available options and accessories, making the matching of boat to trailer relatively painless for the boater. Sometimes even today a boatowner comes by his trailer that way. More often though, new boats come with a trailer as part of the manufacturer's or dealer's package.

Whether you choose a trailer yourself or have the choice made for you, getting the best trailer for your boat and your boating still requires considering and balancing a number of factors before sealing the deal. In addition to the style and size of boat, these include where you go boating and the ramp conditions you expect to encounter there. As always, we'll begin by examining the ratings and what they mean.

TRAILER RATINGS

At the risk of stating the obvious, the trailer you choose must have sufficient load-carrying capacity for the boat you're hauling. Federal law and guidelines set forth by the National Marine Manufacturers Association (NMMA), to which many boat trailer manufacturers belong, require every boat trailer to have a capacity plate that lists not only the trailer identification number but all of the trailer's vital statistics. One of those numbers is the gross trailer weight rating (GTWR), which is the weight of the trailer and boat, the fuel and water, and all the accessories and gear carried inside the boat. In other words, everything north of the pavement.

Let's look at an example of how much a trailer can carry. A Loadmaster Trailer Company Model 210T314CB trailer, designed for hauling heavy 20- to 22-foot boats, has two 3,500-pound-capacity axles and 14-inch "C" load-range tires, giving it a GTWR of 7,000 pounds. The trailer itself weighs 1,381 pounds, so the trailer can carry a maximum of 5,619 pounds of boat, gear, and supplies. If you have installed any accessories on the trailer—such as steps or load guides, which we'll look at below—add in those weights too. It's not unusual for a new boat buyer to wind up with a trailer that has a GTWR that just covers the trailer, boat, and engine. But weight adds up quickly in a boat, as we saw in Chapter 2. Water weighs 8.3 pounds per gallon, so if your boat has an onboard water tank containing, say, 10 gallons, that's 83 pounds. Forty gallons of gasoline weigh 248 pounds. When all is said and done, it's too easy to be overweight.

If you're matching a trailer to your boat, select one with enough load capacity so that the weight of the trailer and loaded boat is no more than 85 percent of the GTWR. So if the trailer capacity plate lists a GTWR of 4,500 pounds, and the trailer itself weighs 800 pounds, the loaded boat on the trailer should weigh no more than 3,025 pounds.

Another load rating listed on every trailer is the gross axle weight rating (GAWR), which is the maximum weight each axle can support safely. For example, if the GAWR on a single-axle trailer is 3,500 pounds, the axle should carry no more than that load, which includes the weight of the axle itself, the trailer, and the boat on the trailer. The trailer may weigh 500 pounds (again, including the axle), so that leaves 3,000 pounds for boat and gear if you were inclined to load the axle to its maximum safe limits.

The same principle holds true for double- and triple-axle trailers. On a tandem-axle trailer, each axle must be rated for at least 2,400 pounds in order to carry a trailer-boat-and-gear load weighing 4,800 pounds.

Boat trailer axles typically range in GAWR between 2,200 and 5,200 pounds. The boat and trailer manufacturers install whatever axle, or axles, that will accommodate the load indicated on the trailer specifications and rating tag. A common practice in the boating world is to place tandem axles on trailers carrying boats that weigh more than 3,000 pounds or are longer than 20 feet.

See the table opposite for typical weights and GAWRs for a variety of trailer types.

GAWR is also an indicator of the minimum tire load rating needed for that axle. An axle with 3,500 pounds capacity must be equipped with tires that can safely support at least 1,750 pounds each when properly inflated. This is easy enough to check by looking at the load rating molded into the tires' sidewall.

Overloaded axles tend to bend or break, overloaded brakes tend to burn up, and overloaded tires tend to disintegrate at the most inopportune times. So, when you are buying new tires for your boat trailer, make sure the tire is specially made for trailer duty, which will be designated by *ST* (or special trailer service) markings on the sidewall. You'll also want to ensure that the tire's load capacity (also listed on the

Table 4.1 — TYPICAL TRAILER WEIGHTS AND CAPACITIES (in pounds/kilograms), BY MATERIAL OF CONSTRUCTION, NUMBER OF AXLES, AND BOAT LENGTH

Material	Boat Length (in feet)	Single-Axle Trailers			Double-Axle Trailers			Triple-Axle Trailers		
		Load Capacity	GAWR	Trailer Weight	Load Capacity	GAWR	Trailer Weight	Load Capacity	GAWR	Trailer Weight
STEEL	10–12	1,000/453	1,200/544	200/90						
	12–14	1,350/612	1,600/725	250/113						
	14–16	1,500/680	2,000/907	350/158						
	16–18	1,850/839	2,400/1,088	460/208	3,500/1,587	4,200/1,905	700/317			
	18–20	2,400/1,088	3,000/1,360	575/260	3,800/1,724	4,650/2,109	800/363	6,500/2,948	7,900/3,583	1,400/635
	22–24	3,200/1,451	4,500/2,041	750/340	4,400/1,996	5,600/2,540	1,150/522	7,000/3,175	8,700/3,946	1,650/748
	24–26	4,500/2,041	5,500/2,494	990/449	5,894/2,674	7,500/3,402	1,530/694	7,400/3,356	9,200/4,163	1,780/807
	26–28	5,000/2,267	6,500/2,948	1,050/476	6,725/3,050	8,600/3,901	1,860/844	10,300/4,672	12,400/5,625	2,100/952
	28–30	5,500/2,494	6,600/2,993	1,090/494	7,400/3,356	9,300/4,218	1,900/862	125,00/5,670	15,200/6,895	2,700/1,225
ALUMINUM	10–12	1,000/453	1,225/556	225/102						
	12–14	1,950/884	2,500/1,134	475/215						
	14–16	2,690/1,221	3,250/1,474	550/249						
	16–18	2,900/1,315	3,500/1,588	585/249						
	18–20	3,200/1,451	3,800/1,724	600/272	4,425/2,007	4,900/2,223	940/426			
	22–24	4,925/2,234	5,900/2,676	926/420	5,680/2,576	6,780/3,075	1,086/493	6,500/2,948	7,025/3,186	1,150/522
	24–26	6,350/2,880	7,000/3,175	1,320/599	6,460/2,930	7,050/3,198	1,248/566	7,480/3,393	7,800/3,538	1,240/562
	26–28	6,600/2,994	8,000/3,628	1,387/629	6,520/2,957	7,800/3,538	1,280/581	8,500/3,855	8,720/3,955	1,280/581
	28–30	7,500/3,402	8,275/3,753	1,679/761	8,500/3,855	10,200/4,627	1,650/748	10,500/4,763	12,500/5,669	2,000/907

Source: Peter duPre/Autoword

NOTE:

The figures are averages; weights & capacities may vary considerably between trailer manufacturers.

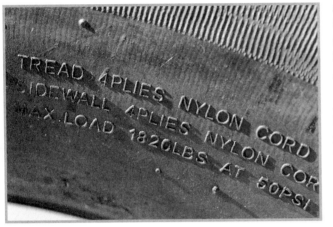

Trailer tires are marked with their load rating and proper inflation pressure.

sidewall) is at least half of the GAWR. Using tires that don't have the proper load range or exceeding the axle-weight carrying capacity is a fast track to a trailer breakdown.

TRAILER TYPES

Apart from its load-carrying capacity, the biggest factor in choosing the right trailer for your boat and application is the manner in which the trailer supports the boat. Boat manufacturers that supply trailers as part of a package spend a lot of time making sure the trailer's hull supports are a perfect match to the boat's size and shape.

Trailers support boats by one of two types of components: flat, carpeted boards or rails, called *bunks*, or *rollers* (also, occasionally and confusingly, called *roller bunks*). Some trailers have a combination of bunks and rollers.

The photo below also illustrates the difference in tongue types that distinguishes some trailers from others. Trailers with the coupler mounted at the end of a single, long tongue are called pole-tongue trailers. Those that support the coupler on forward extensions of both of the trailer's side rails are A-frame trailers. The lightest-weight trailers are pole-tongue trailers, while heavier-duty trailers may be of either design.

Bunk Trailers

I have always been partial to bunk or bunk-and-roller boat trailers because the areas I frequent have fairly decent boat ramps with fairly relaxed regulations that allow me to power my boat onto the trailer with the motor. So I'm able to avoid the more strenuous and inconvenient routine of getting off the boat, hooking up a winch strap to the bow eye, and using muscle and winch to get the boat on the bunks.

Bunks should be covered with carpet to protect the boat's hull and to provide a slippery surface on which to slide the boat. The carpet is slipperiest when wet, so be sure to back the trailer far enough into the water to wet the carpet before either launching or retrieving.

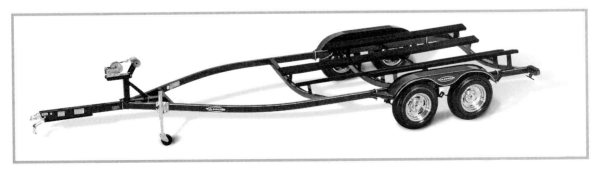

A double-axle, A-frame trailer with carpeted bunks to support the boat. (TRACKER MARINE)

Bunk trailers are less expensive than roller trailers, and those long, carpeted boards support and cradle the entire length of a hull, keeping it well protected from the bounces and shocks encountered during trailering.

The bunks on some trailers are adjustable for height, side-to-side, and fore-and-aft positions, while others are fixed in one or more of these directions. We'll look at this issue later.

Roller Trailers

Some pleasure and sportfishing boats are just too big and heavy for loading and retrieving with a bunk trailer, and some boat ramps ban power-loading, which means either floating the boat on and off the trailer (which, in turn, means backing it somewhat deeper into the water) or using the winch to do the work. And some fresh- and saltwater boat ramps are simply too shallow, too steep, too unimproved, or in such poor shape that power-loading or trying to float a boat onto a trailer isn't practical or it could harm the boat or engine.

That's where trailers with rollers work best. These trailers command a premium price because of all the added hardware, costing sometimes 30 percent more than an equivalent bunk trailer, but the added cost amply justifies itself under the right conditions.

The low-friction rubber or plastic-faced rollers come in different configurations: set in fixed positions on the trailer, attached to articulated channels, placed on adjustable brackets in lieu of carpeted board bunks, or configured in some combination of these. The rollers provide very little resistance, making it easy to slide a boat on and off the trailer—sometimes too easy.

I once witnessed a group of boaters who appeared to be in their twenties readying a 24-foot sport cruiser for a day of play on Lake Mead, near Las Vegas. The boat was on a roller trailer, color-matched and decked out to match both the boat and the Ford dually that was towing it. Everything appeared brand new, and the antics of this crew at the ramp suggested that this outing was one of their first. After a good deal of fiddling around, they got the boat ready to launch. Unfortunately, one of their party decided to help by unhooking the bow strap before his friend started backing down the ramp. As soon as the driver backed the trailer onto the downslope of the ramp, the boat started heading toward the lake faster than the trailer.

When everyone started yelling, the driver hit the brakes which was of course the wrong move. (It's unclear what the right move would have been at this point, short of stepping on the gas in reverse to keep pace with the escaping boat, which might have wound up compounding the mishap!) The boat's transom and the engine's lower unit hit the pavement with a grinding thud.

Luckily, the bow stayed perched on the trailer. Eventually they got the winch strap reattached to the bow eye and, with bystanders pushing on the transom, cranked the boat back onto the trailer. There was evident damage to the hull and lower unit, but not enough to keep them from continuing their adventure on the lake. I wasn't around to see how the retrieval process turned out.

Such mishaps are not uncommon with first-time owners of roller-bunk trailers. In the rush to launch, it's easy to forget that rollers are designed to move the boat on and off the trailer with the utmost of ease. Unlike bunk trailers, in which a certain amount of friction helps to keep the boat on the trailer, only the bow strap and the tie-downs secure a boat on a roller-type trailer.

On the other hand, I have watched a boater retrieve a 30-foot, 10,000-pound boat on a paved ramp merely by running the winch cable out to the boat's bow eye and pulling it up on his roller trailer in a matter of seconds.

On another occasion, I watched a fisherman retrieve a 17-foot, double-ended aluminum drift boat over a gravel riverbank in the same fashion. Both boats glided onto their respective trailers with ease, whereas getting them onto carpeted bunks in the same situations would have been more difficult.

Bunk-and-Roller Trailers

There are a variety of configurations of bunk-and-roller trailers, each with a specific purpose. Some bunk trailers feature a single keel roller on the trailer's rear cross member to help center the boat as it is winched or driven onto the trailer. The roller also bears the greater part of the boat's weight as the boat is winched up and over the sharp ends of the bunks during retrieval. This greatly relieves what would otherwise be a concentration of force on a very small area of the hull—a force strong enough to possibly crack the gelcoat and even do structural damage to a fiberglass hull. The roller is especially helpful on a very shallow ramp or when the trailer hasn't been backed deeply enough into the water.

Some trailers have two rollers, one at each end of the trailer frame, to help protect the boat's keel as it slides off or onto the trailer. The weight of the boat is transferred to the padded bunks when the keel clears the rollers.

Then there are boat trailers that feature a combination of *keel rollers* down the centerline of the trailer, where the boat's keel will rest, and conventional bunks on the outer edges. This design eases loading, while the padded bunks provide broad, even support along the outer edges of the hull bottom and sides. Other combinations of rollers and carpeted bunks are also available.

This trailer features a combination of solidly mounted bunks and keel rollers on a lifting mechanism. The rollers make it easy to get the boat onto and off the trailer. Once they're lowered, the full-length bunks keep the hull well supported.
(RANGER BOATS)

FITTING A TRAILER TO A BOAT

Bunk and Roller Positioning

Not only does a trailer have to be able to carry its load safely and easily, it has to support the boat where the support is needed. Improper trailer fitting or positioning of either carpeted-board bunks or rollers can cause hull deformation on aluminum and fiberglass boats alike, which can seriously degrade the boat's performance and safety. Repairing a deformed hull is a time-consuming, costly process—often to the point of not being cost effective. In other words, if you deform your hull, you may have effectively killed your boat.

The vast majority of today's trailerable boats have hulls of fiberglass or aluminum, formed around a grid of stiffeners. The grid consists of longitudinal *stringers* running from bow to stern, which are interconnected by frames or cross braces. This combination stiffens the hull and keeps its shape smooth and undistorted.

Ideally, you want each trailer bunk to bear against the hull at a strong point—directly beneath a stringer or on the flat side of a *lifting strake* (one of those long fore-and-aft ridges on the bottom of the hull).

Bunks should support the hull under its strong points. The inboard bunks here are directly beneath stringers—that's good. The outboard bunks, however, are beneath unreinforced, flat hull sections—not so good. They should be beneath the triangular lifting strakes. (RANGER BOATS)

Boat positioning relative to bunk alignment is especially critical on trailers with roller-type bunks, because the force of each roller against the hull is concentrated in a small area of contact rather than spread over the length of long, flat, carpeted boards. If the rollers are improperly positioned, the hull can become dimpled over time and possibly even damaged if the trailer were to hit a bump too hard.

Note that any boat with any amount of V in its hull sections—whether riding on rollers, board bunks, or a combination—should bear the majority of its weight on or near its keel (i.e., its fore-and-aft centerline). On many properly set up trailers, it may appear that all the bunks touching the hull are supporting it equally, but that's often not the case. The innermost bunks typically carry most of the load, while the outer bunks serve more to balance the boat and hold it upright.

This is why you should pay close attention to the condition of the inner bunks and rollers when doing your semiannual walk-around trailer inspection. Those bunks are the ones most likely to show the first signs of wear, tear, and mispositioning.

Because bunk/roller positioning is so critical to the health of your boat, it is best to buy a trailer that is designed specifically for your particular make and model of boat. Doing so eliminates problems arising from having the hull supported in the wrong places. Although many bunks and rollers can be adjusted for position, making such changes without understanding the structure of the boat and how it was engineered for trailering can do more harm than good. If you suspect that the hull is not being properly supported, it is best to consult with a trailer specialist, who may have access to the boatbuilder's trailer specifications.

Balancing the Load

Another criterion when choosing the right trailer for your boat is finding one that will balance the boat properly. You want 5 to 10 percent of the trailer's loaded weight resting on the hitch ball. Too much TW on the hitch ball might overload the rear of the tow vehicle, which could adversely affect steering, braking, and handling. Too little TW, on the other hand, can actually lift up the rear of a tow vehicle, causing the trailer to sway the back of the tow vehicle from side-to-side (sometimes called wagging the dog).

The winch stand and its bow stop control the boat's location on the trailer. Some trailers offered in packages have the winch stand welded in just the right location to provide the necessary TW. The problem with this, however, is that it is based on the manufacturer's assumptions of how the boat is loaded and equipped. If you change engines, or load more gear fore or aft than the manufacturer anticipates, the actual TW may change. Unfortunately, it may be difficult or impossible to determine what the manufacturer's assumptions were concerning the distribution of weight in a loaded boat, so your only option would then be to weigh the boat and the tongue, and reposition gear as necessary. (Weighing the tongue is covered below.)

On other trailers, the winch stand is bolted in place, and loosening the nuts allows you to reposition the bow stop a few inches forward (for more TW) or back (for less TW) on the trailer tongue.

The fore-and-aft position of the bow stop, which is bolted to the winch stand, determines the fore-and-aft balance of the load on the trailer.

If your trailer shows signs of wagging the dog, or if your vehicle handles poorly while towing, the likely culprit is too little TW. Check it. If the TW is too low, and your winch stand is adjustable, loosen the winch stand and move it an inch forward or back, then measure again. These small adjustments should be all you need to do if the trailer is a close match to your boat. If your trailer is part of a boat/trailer package with the winch stand attached in a fixed position, take it to your boat dealer for corrective action.

Probably the most convenient way to check TW is take your boat/trailer combo to the local truck scale. Tell the attendant you want to get your trailer's TW. You'll need to ensure only the jack stand is on the scale:

1. Pull up to the scale so the jack stand is over the scale's platform but the trailer's tires are not on the scale.
2. Lower the jack stand and unhitch the trailer.
3. Pull the tow vehicle off the scale so that only the jack stand is on the scale platform.

If you'd rather do it yourself, purchase a scale of your own, such as the Sherline Trailer Tongue Weight Scale. It costs about $110 and measures up to 1,000 pounds (460 kg) within 2 percent accuracy. It looks like a small hydraulic floor jack with an analog gauge. Place the trailer tongue on the scale and you get an instant weight measurement. Simple and fast.

A less expensive alternative is to use a conventional bathroom scale, most of which will weigh up to 300 pounds—in other words, up to 10 percent of a trailer with a 3,000-pound gross vehicle weight rating (GVWR). If you need to weigh more than that, you can use the principle of proportional leverage. Besides the bathroom scale, you'll need a stout board, such as a 2 × 6, about 5 feet long; a block of wood the same thickness as the scale's height; and two pencils or small metal rods:

1. Place the scale on a hard, level surface.
2. Lay one pencil vertically in the middle of the scale.
3. Place a block of wood roughly 4 feet from the scale and lay the second pencil on it. The *pencils* must be exactly 4 feet from each other.
4. Lay the 2 × 6 board on the pencils.
5. Rest the trailer coupler on the 2 × 6 exactly 1 foot from the pencil on the block (i.e., 25 percent of the distance between the two pencils). The trailer frame should be horizontal during this measurement, so if necessary, place a riser of an appropriate height on the 2 × 6 beneath the coupler.
6. At 1 foot from the pencil, the force on the scale will be 75 percent of the TW. For example, 400 pounds of TW will register on the scale as 300 pounds.
7. If you move the coupler 2 feet from the pencil, you'll cut the weight in half, and a 500-pound load will register as 250 pounds.
8. Subtract the weight of the lumber to get the precise TW.
9. Be sure to exercise due caution against having the whole thing topple over on your foot!

By changing the length of the lever arm and adjusting the proportions accordingly, you can measure the TW of any boat trailer you're ever likely to tow.

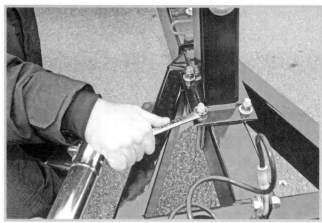

Many winch stands can be easily adjusted fore-and-aft to alter the TW.

AXLE CONFIGURATIONS

Multi-Axle Trailers

As mentioned, boats less than 17 feet long are typically carried on single-axle trailers, while boats 18 feet and longer, or a trailer with a GVWR above 3,000 pounds, may require tandem (dual) axles. Tandem axles support more of the boat's weight, thus decreasing the TW, and this can make the trailer handle better,

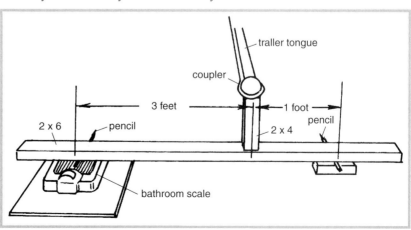

You can use a bathroom scale to measure virtually any boat trailer's TW, even over the scale's 300 pounds maximum, by using a lever to reduce the actual weight on the scale. (JIM SOLLERS)

especially behind a comparatively small, lightweight tow vehicle.

There are a few disadvantages with tandem-axle trailers:

- They are far more difficult to push around by hand than single-axle trailers. If, for example, the parking spot in your garage requires the trailer to be backed in and then pushed sideways and deeper into the garage to close the garage door, a tandem trailer will make this task difficult.
- Tandem-axle trailers cut more to the inside of a turn than their single-axle counterparts. This requires some adjustment in how you drive, although it is not difficult to get used to it. One of the cardinal rules of towing is to know how the trailer reacts and to compensate accordingly—in this case, to take the turns a little wider.
- Many states require brakes on all axles for trailers with GVWRs above certain amounts. In Louisiana, for example, brakes are required on both axles of a tandem trailer with a GVWR of 5,000

You can easily and safely tow most boats up to about 17 feet on a single-axle trailer. Above that figure and you'll usually need tandem axles. (PETER DUPRE; BRUCE W. SMITH)

pounds or more. Obviously, twice as many brakes will increase the cost of the trailer, but before you write this off as a complete disadvantage, bear in mind that a tandem trailer with brakes on both axles provides double the stopping power.

It's often necessary to swing particularly wide around corners when towing a tandem-axle trailer. They cut closer to the insides of turns than single-axle trailers.

On the other hand, if you suffer a flat tire on a tandem-axle trailer and have no spare available, you can remove the flat, lash the wheel-less side of the axle to the trailer frame, and drive to the nearest tire store on your remaining axle. Try doing that with a single-axle trailer!

If you have the option of choosing a single- or tandem-axle boat trailer, I recommend you choose the tandem, especially for a boat over 18 feet long that weighs more than 2,000 pounds loaded and ready to hit the water. I further recommend spending the extra dollars for brakes on each axle, even if not required by state regulations.

Triple-Axle Trailers

The vast majority of first-time trailer boaters won't be towing a boat big enough to require a triple-axle trailer. Triple axles are the norm on trailers designed for boats more than 30 feet in length, with wet weights of more than 8,000 pounds. These include cabin cruisers, sport yachts, and racing-style powerboats.

Triple axles, including triple sets of tires and springs, are needed to distribute the weight of boats of this size, and two or three sets of brakes are needed to bring this much mass to a halt safely. Triple axles provide a bigger footprint and greater stability, which is beneficial given the high center of gravity of many of these boats.

Triple-axle trailers are a real handful, but they're necessary to haul the largest, heaviest trailerable boats.

Naturally, there are some drawbacks:

- Forget about muscling a triple-axle trailer around the parking lot at the boat ramp or into its storage position at home. A tow vehicle is required to even budge these monsters.
- Triple-axle trailers track even more to the inside of turns than tandem-axles.
- Triple-axle trailers respond very slowly to steering input while backing and require a lot of open space to turn. It takes practice to maneuver them efficiently at and around boat ramps.

SUSPENSIONS

Spending most of my life in rural America has given me a great appreciation for a smooth, comfortable ride—especially with a trailer in tow. I don't particularly care for having my innards jostled about with every bump, dip, pothole, or rough stretch of road that passes beneath the tires, and I imagine that most boats don't either. Follow along behind someone towing a boat trailer, and you'd be amazed at how rough the ride is for the boat and everything in it. Batteries, electronics, personal items, fishing rods and tackle, and coolers are all subjected to the same jouncing and jostling. And a rough ride for the trailer can mean a rough ride in the tow vehicle.

Compared with those on our tow vehicles, boat trailer suspensions are rudimentary. The basic trailer suspension consists of nothing more than a pair of leaf springs bolted between the frame and axle. This arrangement provides no shocks to control the leaf springs' up-and-down flexing and frighteningly little travel to dampen the blows as the tires encounter rocks, ruts, speed bumps, and other assorted road irregularities.

Trailer tires are of some help. As the first line of defense in any vehicle suspension, the softer and more pliant the tires are, the more they absorb road-induced impacts. But boat trailer tires are nearly always inflated to their maximum load capacity, which makes them more like rocks than cushy rubber donuts rolling down the road. If the tires are underinflated, they can cause the trailer to bounce around, making matters even worse.

That puts the entire burden for suspension, such as it is, on the springs. If the trailer builder uses springs that closely match the maximum GVWR of the trailer, and the boat you are hauling is close to the trailer's maximum load capacity, the ride will be softer on your boat than if the trailer springs are heavy duty and the boat light.

The good news is that if you don't like your trailer's ride, there are some suspension options that can make life easier and smoother on both your boat and trailer.

Add Your Own Shocks

Shock absorbers slow down and dampen the compression and rebound of the springs. This helps keep the tires on the road surface and also reduces the bouncing of the trailer frame on the axles, resulting in a smoother ride all around. Most trailer manufacturers do not install shocks, however, believing that most buyers are not willing to pay the extra cost.

That leaves it up to the aftermarket to provide trailer owners with a solution, and the aftermarket has stepped up to the plate. One manufacturer, Monroe, offers a bolt-on retrofit kit that includes Monroe RV shock absorbers. The kit starts at around $140 per axle for the lightest trailers. Getting the right retrofit kit and shocks for your boat trailer takes a little measuring and figuring, but installation is easy, requiring nothing more elaborate than drilling a couple of holes and bolting the shock and brackets in place between the trailer frame and axle.

Torsion Axles

Another axle suspension option—one that may eventually replace the decades-old leaf-spring arrangement as the accepted standard—is a rubberized *torsion*

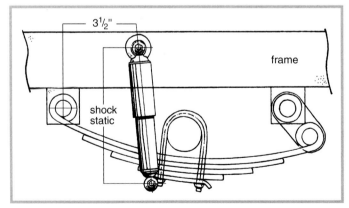

Basic trailer suspension with a shock used to control spring deflection rate.

axle. Torsion axles are already standard on some boat trailers and upgrade options on others.

Rubberized torsion axles are basically an inexpensive way to give a trailer independent suspension. Each wheel is attached to its own axle shaft, called a torsion bar, which may be square or triangular in cross section. The torsion bar is cushioned and held in place in the axle housing by a block of solid rubber or individual rubber cords. The wheel hub is mounted on a lever arm on the outer end of the torsion bar. As road irregularities force the lever arm up and down, the rotation of the shaft is controlled, sprung, and dampened by the rubbers.

I hope never again to own a boat trailer with a leaf-spring suspension, a conclusion I came to the first time I towed two identical boats. They were 20-foot bass boats—one loaded on a standard leaf-sprung trailer, the other on a trailer equipped with a torsion-axle suspension. The torsion suspension was smoother and more stable; so much so, it felt like towing two completely different boats.

Rubberized torsion-axle assemblies are available to fit trailers with load capacities from as little as 500 pounds per axle to more than 8,000 pounds per axle. They're also available as retrofit kits for as little as $250 per axle. This is good news for owners of boat trailers that have leaf-spring suspensions, and it may be worth the cost if you plan to keep an existing trailer another five or ten years. Installation takes a fair amount of skill, knowledge, and professional tools, however, so you might have to add in the cost of professional installation.

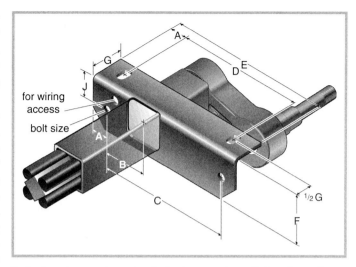

Torsion-bar axles are a step up from leaf-spring suspensions, offering a degree of damping without shock absorbers. (DEXTER AXLE CORPORATION)

BRAKES

The combination of boat and trailer will frequently weigh nearly as much, if not more, than the tow vehicle. As such, trailer brakes comprise the single most important component of trailer safety aft of the trailer hitch.

The reason is simple: a tow vehicle's brakes are designed to stop just the tow vehicle, not the tow vehicle and what it is towing. To be safe, you must not only bring the boat trailer to a stop, but also do so within a safe distance for the speed at which your vehicle is traveling—for example, within 25 feet when traveling at 20 mph. Wyoming, Oregon, New Jersey, Missouri, and several other states have codified such a requirement in their vehicle laws.

In addition to performance requirements, most states have equipment requirements concerning trailer brakes. For example:

- California and Tennessee require trailer brakes on at least one axle on trailers weighing more than 1,500 pounds.
- North Dakota requires brakes on all trailers regardless of size when towed above 25 mph.
- Idaho, Mississippi, and Ohio require brakes on trailers weighing more than 2,000 pounds.

In addition, federal law mandates brakes on virtually all trailers with a gross trailer weight (GWT) of more than 3,000 pounds, and the American Boat & Yacht Council (ABYC) recommends brakes on all boat trailers above 1,500 pounds.

This means that unless you are towing an aluminum or fiberglass boat that's shorter than 16 or 17 feet—or a small sailboat such as a Laser, Sunfish, or similar—your trailer may be required to have brakes on at least one axle. In fact, I feel it's prudent that every trailer that weighs more than 1,000 pounds when loaded should have its own brakes, even if the regulations in your state don't require them.

The responsibility for complying with the law in your state is yours. You should learn your state regulations, and don't assume that your braking system is legal simply because you bought the trailer in-state. Boat trailer manufacturers don't build trailers to meet every state's towing laws.

The table opposite lists the basic requirements for braking systems, along with several other important trailering stipulations, by state and province. But this table is a summary only, and it is believed to be accurate only at the time of this writing: state laws change so often and vary so widely that it's impossible to include all pertinent details. Therefore, it's essential that you get the most detailed and up-to-date information directly from your state's department of motor vehicles (see Appendix B).

Boat trailer brakes fall into three basic categories. In order of descending popularity—though not necessarily of effectiveness—these are hydraulic surge, electric, and electric/hydraulic. Nine times out of ten, the boat trailer you buy will be equipped with hydraulic surge brakes—not because they are the best, but because they are perceived as being the most trouble-free.

Hydraulic Surge Brakes

The hydraulic surge braking system has been used on the majority of boat trailers for the past 50 years because it is reliable, simple, and effective. The system is self-contained and automatic, requiring no electric or hydraulic connection from the tow vehicle to apply the trailer brakes. When the tow vehicle slows down relative to the trailer, the trailer tongue pushes against the hitch and coupler. A pawl inside the coupler activates the trailer's master brake cylinder in a manner similar to what happens when you exert pressure on the brake pedal in the tow vehicle. This pressurizes the hydraulic fluid in the cylinder and brake lines, pushing the brake shoes against the drums and slowing the trailer. (This describes drum brakes, which are the more common type. In the case of disc brakes, simply change *shoes* for *pads*, and *drums* for *discs*, and the explanation still holds.)

The elegance and simplicity of a surge-brake system is that the mechanical pressure created by the coupler pressing against the hitch ball is proportional to the difference in deceleration between the tow vehicle and the trailer. Therefore the hydraulic output of the brake coupler, and the resulting brake operation, is automatically proportional to the amount of braking applied by the tow vehicle.

There are, however, several downsides inherent in hydraulic surge brake design. One, as we've already seen, is that they are incompatible with weight-distributing systems and anti-sway bars (Chapter 3).

Another downside is that the trailer brakes will lock if you try to back your trailer up any kind of incline. Needless to say, this can be a real annoyance. To override it on older or less sophisticated trailers, you have to disable the coupler so that it doesn't slide back into the surge brake master cylinder. You can buy a special clip for this purpose from just about any boat dealer.

Table 4.2 TOWING LAWS BY U.S. STATE AND CANADIAN PROVINCE

STATE OR PROVINCE	Max. Trailer Length (in feet)	Max. Trailer Width (in feet)	Max. Trailer Height (in feet)	Max. Overall Length (in feet)	Weight Trailer Brakes Req. (in pounds)	Max. Towing Speed (mph)
Alabama	40	8	13.6	60	3,000	55
Alaska	40	8	13.6	65	3,000	55
Arizona	40	8	13.6	65	3,000	55
Arkansas	40	8	13.6	65	3,000	60
California	40	8.6	14	65	1,500 (3,000 for boat trailers)	55
Colorado	35	8.6	13	70	3,000	65
Connecticut	45	8.6	13.6	60	3,000	55
Delaware	40	8.6	13.6	60	4,000	55
District of Columbia	40	8	13.6	65	3,000	55
Florida	48	8.6	13.6	65	3,000	65
Georgia	n/a	8	13.6	60	2,500	55
Hawaii	40	9	13.6	65	3,000	50
Idaho	45	8.6	14	65	1,500	65
Illinois	42	8	13.6	60	3,000	55
Indiana	40	8.6	13.6	60	3,000	55
Iowa	48	8.6	13.6	65	3,000	60
Kansas	45	8.6	14	65	n/a	55
Kentucky	n/a	8	13.6	55	n/a	60
Louisiana	40	8	13.6	70	3,000	55
Maine	45	8.6	13.6	65	3,000	65
Maryland	n/a	8.6	13.6	55	3,000	65
Massachusetts	40	8.6	13.6	65	n/a	55
Michigan	45	8	13.6	60	3,000	55
Minnesota	48	8	13.6	65	3,000	65
Mississippi	50	8.6	13.6	70	2,000	65
Missouri	40	8	14	65	n/a	65
Montana	n/a	8.6	14	75	3,000	n/a
Nebraska	40	8.6	14.6	65	3,000	65
Nevada	40	8.6	14	70	1,500	65
New Hampshire	48	8	13.6	60	3,000	65
New Jersey	35	8	13.6	50	3,000	55
New Mexico	40	8.6	14	65	3,000	65
New York	45	8.6	13.6	65	3,000	65
North Carolina	40	8.6	13.6	60	4,000	55

(continued)

Table 4.2 TOWING LAWS BY U.S. STATE AND CANADIAN PROVINCE (continued)

STATE OR PROVINCE	Max. Trailer Length (in feet)	Max. Trailer Width (in feet)	Max. Trailer Height (in feet)	Max. Overall Length (in feet)	Weight Trailer Brakes Req. (in pounds)	Max. Towing Speed (mph)
North Dakota	60	8.6	14	75	all	65
Ohio	40	8.6	13.6	65	2,000	55
Oklahoma	40	8.6	13.6	65	3,000	65
Oregon	45	8.6	13.6	65	n/a	55
Pennsylvania	n/a	8	13.6	60	3,000	55
Rhode Island	48	8.6	13.6	60	4,000	55
South Carolina	48	8.6	13.6	n/a	3,000	55
South Dakota	53	8.6	14	70	3,000	65
Tennessee	48	8.6	13.6	65	3,000	65
Texas	n/a	8.6	13.6	65	4,500	55
Utah	48	8.6	14	65	2,000	65
Vermont	45	8.6	13.6	60	3,000	55
Virginia	40	8.6	13.6	60	3,000	55
Washington	48	8.6	14	75	3,000	60
West Virginia	40	8	13.6	65	3,000	55
Wisconsin	45	8.6	13.6	65	3,000	65
Wyoming	60	8.6	14	65	3,000	60

CANADA	Max. Trailer Length (feet/ meters)	Max. Trailer Width (feet/ meters)	Max. Trailer Height (feet/ meters)	Max. Overall Length (feet/ meters)	Weight Trailer Brakes Req. (pounds/ kilograms)	Max. Towing Speed (mph/kph)
Alberta	41/12.5	8.5/2.6	12.6/3.85	66/20	2,004/909	n/a
British Columbia	41/12.5	8.5/2.6	12.6/3.85	66/20	3,087/1,400	n/a
Manitoba	41/12.5	8.5/2.6	13.6/4.15	70.5/21.5	2,007/910	n/a
New Brunswick	41/12.5	8.5/2.6	13.6/4.15	75.5/23	3,300/1,500	n/a
Newfoundland	41/12.5	8.5/2.6	13.5/4.1	75.5/23	9.923/4,500	n/a
NWT—Nunavut	41/12.5	8.5/2.6	13.6/4.15	80/25	2,998/1,360	n/a
Nova Scotia	48.1/14.65	8.5/2.6	13.6/4.15	75/23	3,969/1,800	n/a
Ontario	41/12.5	8.5/2.6	13.6/4.15	75/23	2,998/1,360	n/a
Prince Edward Isl.	53.2/16.2	8.5/2.6	13.6/4.15	75.5/23	2,977/1,350	n/a
Quebec	53.2/16.2	8.5/2.6	13.6/4.15	75/23	2,867/1,300	n/a
Saskatchewan	41/12.5	8.5/2.6	13.6/4.15	75/23	2,977/1,350	n/a
Yukon	53/16	8.2/2.5	13.7/4.2	82/25	2,007/910	n/a

NOTE:
Towing laws are subject to change. Check with the relevant authorities to confirm current regulations (see Appendix B).

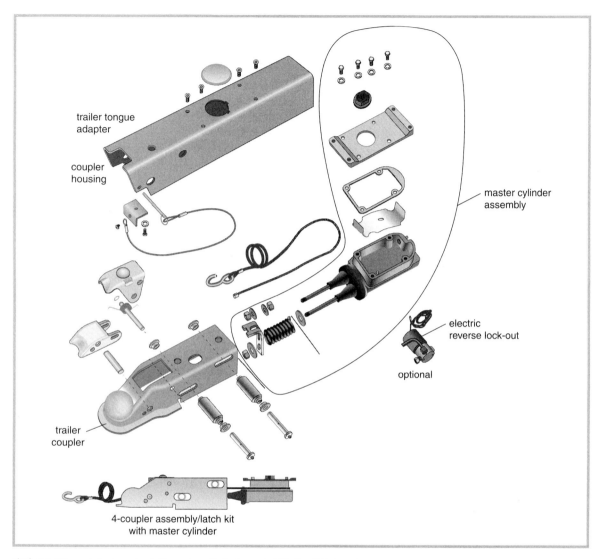

trailer tongue
adapter

coupler
housing

master cylinder
assembly

electric
reverse lock-out

optional

trailer
coupler

4-coupler assembly/latch kit
with master cylinder

The heart of the surge brake system is the master cylinder housed within the sliding coupler. (TRAILER BOATS/FULTON PERFORMANCE PRODUCTS)

Many of the newer surge brake systems—particularly those designed for disc brakes—come with an electric override. As soon as the tow vehicle's backup lights come on, a solenoid in the coupler bypasses the flow of hydraulic fluid in the brake line away from the wheel cylinders, disengaging the braking system. This system uses a five-pin trailer wiring harness, rather than the standard four-pin. The fifth pin ties into the tow vehicle's backup lights and electrically disengages the surge brake system whenever reverse gear is engaged.

A bigger concern with hydraulic surge brakes is that the trailer brakes won't work when the trailer is doing the pulling, as when backing down a steep boat ramp or when you are parked on a hill. This can be a big problem when the

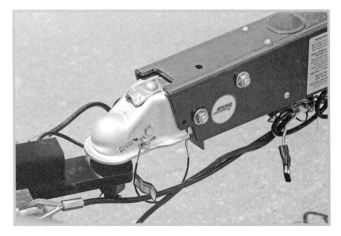

Surge brakes are simple, effective, and inexpensive. Their main problem is incompatibility with weight-distributing hitches and anti-sway bars.

boat/trailer package weighs more than the tow vehicle or when the brakes on the tow vehicle are not very effective.

As of this writing, hydraulic surge brakes still dominate the market, but don't be surprised if they are replaced entirely by electric trailer brakes within the next few years.

Electric Brakes

Although electric braking systems have been used on utility and RV trailers for decades, they haven't found great acceptance by the boating public. Besides concerns over their high initial cost, many boaters believe electric brakes are unreliable in a marine environment.

That may have been true 20 years ago, but times—and technology—have changed. Prices of electric brake components have dropped, and old problems of corroded wiring, connections, and electric brake solenoids have been thoroughly sorted out by the brake manufacturers. Modern electric trailer brakes—such as Fulton Performance Products' Ful-Stop system—have components and connections that are reportedly waterproof and submersible. Electric boat trailer braking systems are now legal in all fifty states and becoming increasingly popular among the better boat trailer manufacturers. Custom boat trailer builders such as Loadmaster Trailer Company and EZ Loader Boat Trailers are installing them on more and more trailers. Electric brakes represent the future of boat trailer brake systems.

Electronic controllers allow electric trailer brakes to be activated manually and to be adjusted for braking power. (LARRY WALTON)

The mechanical side of an electric brake system is pretty much the same as in a hydraulic surge brake system. The difference is in the actuation. When the driver steps on the brake pedal, an electronic brake controller installed in the tow vehicle activates the trailer's brakes. This effectively joins the tow vehicle's and the trailer's brakes into a single system that functions together whether you are moving forward or backing up. This makes a big difference when you are backing a 6,000-pound boat and trailer down a wet, steep boat ramp with a 5,000-pound SUV.

Electric boat trailer brakes operate off the tow vehicle's 12-volt electrical system. The trailer brake wire, which should be black, accounts for one of the five or seven pins in the boat trailer's wiring harness plug. When you step on the brakes, this wire carries electricity to an electromagnet located in the drum brake assembly. As current is applied, the electromagnet moves a lever that forces the brake shoes against the drum, slowing the trailer.

There are three basic styles of electronic brake controllers:

- Timing-activated controller: This is the simplest and least expensive controller and is wired into the tow vehicle's brake light switch. When you apply the tow vehicle's brakes, the trailer's brakes are activated. You can set the controller for the strength of the braking response, but it's a simple on/off function. Pressing harder on the brake pedal won't apply the trailer brakes any harder. This full-on/full-off braking can produce a jerking motion.
- Inertia-activated controller: This controller utilizes a pendulum that senses how rapidly the tow vehicle is stopping and stops the trailer at the same rate.
- Proportional-activated brake controller: This one is the most expensive and sophisticated of the three. It uses an accelerometer instead of a pendulum to measure the g-force of the vehicle stopping, then it applies the trailer brakes accordingly. It is fast, smooth, and expensive—as well as the best on the market.

Electric brakes can be fine-tuned for different trailer weights and road conditions, and they can be operated independently of the tow vehicle's brakes. Should your tow vehicle's brakes go out for any reason, you would be in big trouble trying to stop a boat trailer with surge brakes. With electric brakes, however, you can use the manual slide to apply the trailer brakes, which would eventually help bring the whole rig to a halt. You can also dampen trailer sway and keep the trailer under control by momentarily activating the trailer brakes using the controller. You'll want to find the cause of the sway before you go much farther, but this technique will get you home. Finally, electric brakes are compatible with anti-sway bars and weight-distributing hitches.

The biggest challenge to installing an electronic brake controller is the wiring. The circuit is fairly simple, but if you have no electrical background, it's best left to a professional. Ford and GM have integrated an electric brake controller into the dash of their heavy-duty pickups, effectively taking all of the wiring fuss out of the equation.

Another potential drawback of electric trailer brakes is that it's not as easy to share your trailer with another tow vehicle. If your trailer is equipped with electric brakes, the other tow vehicle must be equipped not only with the right size hitch and hitch ball but also with an electric brake controller that's compatible with your trailer's brakes.

Electric/Hydraulic Brakes

Electric/hydraulic brakes (also known as electric-over-hydraulic brakes) use an electric brake controller, similar to that used in an all-electric system, and hydraulic lines on the trailer to apply braking pressure. Relying on a highly engineered actuator pump to convert the electric signal into hydraulic pressure,

Drum brakes (top) are most often installed as standard equipment. Disc brakes (bottom) cost more, but they're more effective in wet conditions—the very places boat trailers tend to be used. (TRACKER MARINE/RANGER BOATS)

these systems are expensive (often around $1,000). However, they answer all of the concerns of the other systems (i.e., they permit the use of weight-distributing hitches, while keeping the electrical components out of the water). Because of their cost, they are generally found only on large, heavy trailers and seldom on the types of trailers first-time boatowners will be towing.

Discs vs. Drums

Disc brakes are an appealing option over drum brakes. Disc brakes provide better stopping power when subjected to water, dirt, or mud, and they are easier to maintain. If you are really into looks and performance, you can choose stainless steel versions or have the brake calipers and rotors powder coated to match the boat, trailer, and/or tow vehicle.

TRAILER OPTIONS

A basic boat trailer is comparable to a basic tow vehicle. It might not look great or possess the options and accessories that make life on the road as safe, convenient, and comfortable as possible, but it does the job nonetheless.

However, in the same way that consumers buy more tow vehicles with the bells and whistles than they do the stripped-down models, so too they typically buy their boat trailers with manufacturer/dealer options and then later equip them with aftermarket goodies. Let's look at the most popular trailer options.

Trailer Materials and Protection

Boat trailers are constructed from either galvanized or painted steel or aluminum. Steel, being the less expensive option, is far more common, but of course, it is subject to rust in a boating environment. With proper attention, a painted steel trailer can last through many years of freshwater boating—proper attention consisting of watching for rust and addressing it as soon as it makes an appearance. In a marine (i.e., saltwater) environment, however, no amount of attention will protect a

SPECIAL TRAILERS FOR PONTOON BOATS

Pontoon boats, because of their unique hull configuration, require a specialized trailer. These are designed to carry the boat lower to the ground, so the trailer doesn't have to be backed deep into the water for launching and retrieving. To this end, pontoon trailers often have small 10- and 12-inch tires with high load ratings in the D and E range to carry the weight of both trailer and 'toon. Two types of pontoon trailers are common: *float-on* and *raising/lowering* models. A float-on trailer is mechanically simpler and therefore less expensive and more popular. It is designed for use on steeper boat ramps, where the trailer gets deep into the water quickly. This allows the boat to slide on and off with relative ease and without getting the tow vehicle any farther into the water than one would with a conventional boat trailer. Bunks are directly beneath the pontoon *logs*, or they support the underside of the deck, with the logs straddling the supports.

This float-on trailer for a pontoon boat supports the boat's logs. (DAN ARMITAGE)

Raising/lowering pontoon trailers have a mechanism that moves the bunks up and back simultaneously. Activation may be by hand-crank, electric motor, or hydraulics. Because it moves the boat farther aft, this system is preferable for use on shallow boat ramps.

Regardless of trailer type, it is a good idea to equip pontoon trailers with loading guides. (See below for a discussion of loading guides and other trailer options.) Pontoon boats don't have V-hulls that align with the bunks and self-center on the trailer, and the guides make loading far easier, as they help you center the boat on the trailer as you winch or pull it up to the bow stop.

Although double-axle trailers are the most common, triples are increasing in popularity as pontoon boats are now reaching lengths in excess of 36 feet and weights of more than 6,000 pounds. Many pontoon trailers are equipped with electric disc brakes on all axles, because the 7-inch-diameter drum brakes that would normally be on the small wheels may not provide adequate braking for some of the heavier rigs. Many of the pontoon trailer manufacturers I interviewed highly recommend electric disc brakes—an upgrade that

(continued)

typically adds about $300 to the price of a trailer equipped with hydraulic drum brakes. The new electric disc-brake systems are specifically designed for water submersion; they are reliable for boat trailer use and require far less service than conventional drum brakes.

Since the small wheels on pontoon trailers rotate on their axles many more times per mile than the larger ones on conventional boat trailers, it's particularly important to keep the lug nuts tight and the tires at their maximum inflation pressure. Manufacturers typically recommend checking lug-nut tightness every 50 miles for the first 500 miles. After that, check them before every outing—just to be safe. Tire inflation should also be checked on a regular basis. On a 10-inch E-load range tire, the inflation pressure should be 90 pounds per square inch (psi), and on a 12-inch D-load range tire, it's 100 psi. Running tires at a lower pressure could cause the trailer to sway.

painted steel trailer. Galvanized steel then becomes the main choice, although aluminum is an attractive option, too.

One of the newer boat trailer options—quickly becoming standard on upscale steel trailers—is the addition of special coatings on the frame to keep rust and corrosion from getting a foothold in the dings caused by rocks and road debris.

For example, Ranger Boats, a boat manufacturer with one of the largest in-house trailer-building facilities in the country, coats its trailer frames with a rubberized coating called Polyeuro, a product derived from the spray-in bed liners used in pickup trucks. This coating resists chipping and scratching more effectively than conventional paints, galvanizing, and powder-coating processes.

If such a coating isn't available for your trailer, consider any option the manufacturer offers to protect the trailer from the ravages of the elements—especially if salt or brackish water is familiar territory.

Bearing Protectors

Bearing protectors, often referred to by the trade name Bearing Buddy, are among the most popular and useful trailer accessories. A bearing protector is a small, pressurized reservoir of grease that replaces the cap over the axle hub (not the *wheel cover* commonly known by the misnomer *hub cap*, but the small steel cup in the center of the hub that covers the outer wheel bearing). A simple mechanical spring maintains constant pressure against the reserve grease; if any grease weeps from the bearing, it is immediately replaced by fresh grease, thus preventing water or grit from entering the bearing races. Maintenance is easy, requiring no disassembling. You simply refill the reservoir with a grease gun through a zerk fitting.

A more recent development is the oil-bath bearing protector, which keeps the bearings lubricated with oil rather than grease. The clear plastic covers allow you to check oil levels with a mere glance.

For such a simple device, bearing protectors offer tremendous advantages, ensuring that the bearings have adequate lubrication at all times, excluding water and dirt that can cause bearing damage, and reducing maintenance.

Installation is simple:

1. Pry the stock cap off the hub.
2. Press the grease-based bearing protector into place with a rubber mallet or a hammer and a block of wood. (Threaded versions are available to replace threaded caps.)

If the bearings already have a few miles on them, you'll need to do some maintenance before installing the bearing protectors:

1. Disassemble the bearings.
2. Clean and inspect for damage.
3. Thoroughly re-grease the bearings and reassemble.
4. Install the bearing protectors as described above.

Trailer Wheels and Tires

An often-overlooked option is upgrading your trailer wheels and tires to more closely match those of your tow vehicle. In doing so, remember that trailers require special tires designed for trailering, which limits your options. Polished or satin-finished aluminum wheels hold up better and look nicer over the long haul than their chrome counterparts, and you can usually find trailer wheels in a design that matches the wheels on your tow vehicle.

The biggest concern when you select new wheels is to match the size and offset of the original wheels. You don't want the new wheels to interfere with the trailer's brakes or to cause the tires to rub the fenders. Choosing wheels offered by the trailer manufacturer is a safe way to ensure that all is well under the fenders. But if you don't like the wheels offered by the trailer manufacturer, they're readily available from other sources.

Grease-reservoir bearing protectors keep grit and water out of the bearings, significantly reducing maintenance and improving reliability. (BEARING BUDDY, INC.)

The fenders on this trailer are well designed for use as steps, with wide diamond-plated standing surfaces.

Nonskid Walking Surface

Sooner or later, most trailer boaters tire of trying to balance themselves on the narrow and sometimes slippery tongue of the trailer in order to connect the winch strap to the bow eye during the retrieval process. The slightest misstep means wet feet, which in the non-summer months means cold feet.

A nonskid surface on the trailer tongue solves this by providing good traction. In its simplest form, the surface is nothing more than a heavy sandpaper-like tape that's applied to the top of the trailer tongue. This tape also works great on the tops of fenders and on any other part of the trailer you find yourself using as a step to reach into the boat.

A step up (so to speak) from nonskid tape is an auxiliary platform known as a walk ramp or step, which is often made of diamond-plated steel. Bolted to the trailer tongue just in front of the winch stand, this step provides a wider surface upon which to stand as you hook or unhook the bow straps or safety chains.

Many stock fenders are not made for standing or stepping on. Heavy-duty fenders with built-in steps are available, both as options and aftermarket items, and they provide good standing surfaces.

Loading Guides

If you have a big dually or a tow vehicle that partially obscures the view of your boat trailer when you back it down a ramp, getting the proper position on the ramp can be a problem. Likewise, when the rear end of the trailer is underwater, it can be hard for the operator to line up the boat properly on the bunks during retrieval. This can be even more of a problem on a boat with a tall bow, which can make it impossible to see even the winch stand at anything less than about 20 feet distance.

The side guides installed at the rear corners of the trailer help align the boat during retrieval.

Loading guides consist of plastic poles that rise several feet from the rear corners of a trailer. They enable both the tow vehicle driver and the boat operator to see the location of the trailer corners, and thus to execute the launch or retrieval quickly and smoothly.

While the guides mentioned above provide a visual reference, heavier-duty versions are available that physically guide the boat as you float it onto the trailer, helping to center it and keeping it off the trailer fenders. They can also serve as pivot points for levering the boat into position in a crosswind or current. Even when made of metal, they are covered with plastic, to prevent marring the boat's finish. Guides are also available for mounting near the front of the trailer, to help steer the bow of the boat into the bow stop.

You can make loading guides yourself or purchase them. They range in price from less than $75 to more than $150 and are available in different shapes and sizes. If a trailer doesn't come with loading guides, you can get them from a local boat dealer, a marine supplier, or over the Internet.

Guide Lights

If you are ever faced with loading or launching your boat at night—and chances are you will be—you'll appreciate guide lights. A boat trailer can be really hard to see in such situations, making positioning the trailer a challenge for the tow vehicle operator, and getting the boat on the trailer an even bigger challenge for the boat operator. You can install guide lights to your existing loading guides using marine-grade LED (light-emitting diode) lights, or you can buy them in kit form from companies such as Pipe Lights and B&M Products. Mount a single LED light near the top of each loading guide, facing rearward. You should be able to get the trailer pretty well lit up for less than $100, and installation is easy.

For boaters who prefer not to have loading guides because they look, well, funky, B&M Products offers a Guide-Lites kit for less than $25. It consists of a pair of sleek, 2-foot-tall, thin plastic tubes embedded with a row of small LEDs. These little light sticks leave little doubt as to where the corners of your boat trailer are when you're trying to maneuver in the dead of night—plus they look high-tech.

Backup Lights and LED Lights

Another handy upgrade is auxiliary backup lights. These help immensely when you're backing a trailer alongside your garage at night or trying to squeeze it between trees at some unlit lakeside campground. When the only light available is what's coming from your weak trailer and tow vehicle backup lights, your visibility is limited at best.

One approach is to attach a pair of rectangular fog lights to the rear bumper of the tow vehicle and wire them into the tow vehicle's backup light circuit. Such lights provide a much brighter and wider illumination than factory backup lights. If you angle the lights to shine more to the sides than straight back, you'll have light to illuminate the trailer's path during a turn.

Many higher-end boat trailers now come equipped with ultrabright LED backup lights. If your trailer doesn't have them, it's a good idea to make the switch yourself. For example, the 4-inch-diameter Anderson Marine Great White LED Back-Up Lights are superbright and totally submersible.

Where's the trailer? With the load guides sticking up above the water, it's easier to get the boat aligned properly. Note the lights mounted on top of the guides, which will help loading at night.

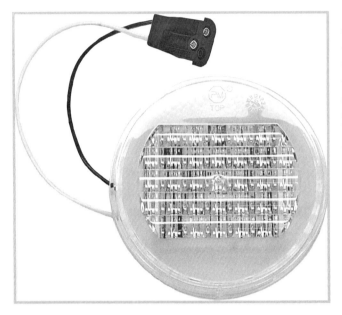

LED backup lights are much brighter than the incandescent models that come standard on most trailers. Plus, they're more durable and water-resistant.
(ANDERSON MARINE)

While you're thinking about lights, it would also be a good idea to upgrade your trailer to LED running lights and multifunction taillights (if it isn't already so equipped) to make the trailer more visible. LEDs have a longer life (as much as 100,000 hours in some applications) than regular trailer bulbs, plus they are brighter than incandescent lights and more resistant to the effects of vibrations and water intrusion.

Tire Pressure Monitoring Systems (TPMS)

Years ago I was in a convoy of boaters headed back to the Los Angles area from a long boating weekend at Lake Mojave, near Las Vegas. We'd been on the road for a couple of hours when a piece of debris suddenly clobbered the front of my truck. A few moments later, from the passenger's side of the tandem-axle boat trailer ahead of me, sparks started spitting out as if a grinder were laying into steel. One of the rear tires on the trailer had blown, and the rim was grinding along on the pavement. The driver had no clue. By the time I'd gotten his attention, and he'd gotten the trailer pulled off the side of the busy interstate, the wheel was toast.

On another occasion, I had to flag down a fellow boater to let him know a tire on his single-axle trailer was nearly flat. He was completely unaware of the situation and would probably have driven until it, too, went completely flat, putting his boat, trailer, and tow vehicle in jeopardy.

It is all too common to see tow vehicles and trailers running on dangerously underinflated tires. One way to keep an eye on both your tow vehicle and boat trailer tire pressures is to install an electronic tire pressure monitoring system. The typical vehicle system uses four air-pressure sensors, one mounted on each wheel rim (before the tire is mounted) or installed in place of the conventional valve stem. Each sensor records tire pressure, and when that pressure drops to a preset level, a tiny transmitter sends a signal to a receiver in the tow vehicle, indicating which tire is low. The same system applies to boat trailers. These systems have been around for a few years and have proven reliable and accurate.

Tire pressure monitors are mandatory on all new 2008 passenger cars and light trucks, and they are available on the aftermarket, many of them costing under $300, for retrofitting to older vehicles. Rosta Precision Controls offers a variety of aftermarket TPMS Kits.

Spare Tire Mount

Unfortunately, most trailer manufacturers offer a spare tire and a mount as an option, not as standard equipment. Buy it.

Spare tire mounts are also available as aftermarket accessories. Some hold the wheel vertical, and others cradle it horizontally between the trailer's rails.

Swing-Away Trailer Tongues and Tongue Extensions

Rare is the garage or carport that is deep enough to accommodate a trailer backed straight in. Much more commonly, the trailer has to be angled in, consuming precious garage space, or you wind up with the trailer tongue jutting out of the carport to trip unwary passers-by or interfere with the garage door closing. The solution to this aggravation is the swing-away or detachable trailer tongue.

These trailer tongues allow you to quickly shorten the trailer's overall length by as much as 2 feet. You simply remove the locking pin or bolt and swing the tongue to the side of the trailer. If the new trailer you are buying doesn't include one, see if you can add it as an option or have one installed by the dealer. They are usually a manufacturer option because each one must be designed for a specific trailer, and they are worth every penny when parking space is at a premium.

Occasionally you'll encounter a boat ramp so shallow that it requires backing the tow vehicle way into the water to get the boat on and off the trailer. A trailer tongue extension comes in handy at such times, keeping the tow vehicle out of the water and off slippery ramp surfaces. Extend-A-Hitch is one manufacturer that offers such extensions. With an Extend-A-Hitch, you can add anywhere from 5 to 10 feet to the length of the trailer tongue once you get to the ramp.

Trailer tongue extensions are bolted to the trailer frame, either alongside the rollers or bunk brackets or beneath the trailer's regular towing tongue. Before launching or retrieving, unhitch your tow vehicle, extend the auxiliary tongue, lock it into place with a locking pin, then hitch your vehicle to the coupler on the tongue extension. Tongue extensions do not incorporate brakes in the couplers, however, and they *are not engineered for highway use*. Use them only for launching and retrieving the boat, then switch back to the trailer's regular coupler before driving away.

Tongue Jacks

Although some trailer makers offer a tongue jack as an option, it is really a necessity

As part of an electronic tire pressure monitoring system, this sensor will be installed on the wheel rim, inside the tire. When tire pressure is too low, it will send a wireless signal to a receiver in the tow vehicle's cab, alerting the driver.

A spare tire is essential. Buy a bracket that allows you to lock the tire securely. (VENTURE TRAILERS/RANGER BOATS)

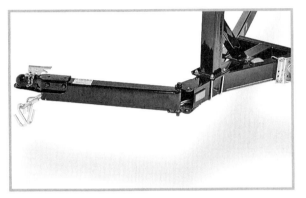

A swing-away trailer tongue shortens the length of the trailer, allowing you to park it in smaller spaces, such as garages and carports. (TRACKER MARINE)

to lift and lower the coupler onto and off of the hitch ball. It's also good for keeping the coupler off the ground when it's not hitched to the ball—since there isn't always a concrete block handy. Most jacks on boat trailers are fitted with a wheel on the bottom, rather than a flat pad, and these are often called tongue dollies. They allow you to roll the boat and trailer around by hand, to the extent that you can move that much weight. Jacks are bolted either to the tongue or to one of the trailer's side rails near the tongue.

A tongue jack operates with a rack-and-pinion mechanism, raising and lowering with either a hand crank or an electric motor. In addition, some jacks also swivel and lock into a horizontal position. In essence, this allows them to be lifted a few inches higher off the ground.

Powered tongue jacks are a nice feature for use with big, heavy boats. The Atwood Mobile Products Power Jack, which sells for around $250 on the Internet and in most large boating accessory stores, is one example of a good-performing jack. It replaces the standard hand-crank unit and attaches to a 12-volt power source—usually a small battery mounted on the trailer. The jack lifts up to 1,000 pounds of tongue weight with the push of a button.

Electric Winches

A similar, 12-volt, muscle-saving device is the electric winch, which replaces the standard hand-crank version. These cost anywhere from $150 to $450, depending on size and brand. Powerwinch, the best-known brand, is available in several sizes to fit a wide range of boats. The company even offers remote-controlled winches so you can stand back several feet as you winch the boat up to the bow stop—a comforting feature if you're worried about possible recoil injury from a broken cable.

The batteries for electric jacks and winches are typically mounted on the trailer tongue where they won't be submerged when launching. Some are wired to be recharged by the tow vehicle's alternator, while others must be periodically hooked up to a battery charger.

Depending upon their pull ratings, winches come equipped with a fiber rope, a strap, or a wire rope or cable. Lighter, smaller boats, up to about 2,000 pounds, often get by with a fiber rope. Winches for boats up to about 7,000 pounds (typically

A trailer tongue extension adds several feet to the length of the trailer, allowing you to back the boat farther into the water without getting your tow vehicle's rear wheel hubs wet. (EXTEND-A-HITCH)

from 20 to 24 feet) often have straps. Boats weighing more than 7,000 pounds should use an electric winch with a wire rope.

Pick a winch that has a pulling (not lifting) capacity rating of at least half the combined weight of your boat, motor, and gear. Boat length is not a reliable indicator of weight.

Brake Flush Kits

Brake components are particularly subject to corrosion, especially if you do your boating in salt water. For example, the inside surface of a brake drum has to be plain, raw steel to work right, which means you can't use paint or galvanization to protect the metal.

But you can protect the insides of your brakes from salt corrosion with a freshwater brake flush kit. Installation is easy: fasten the spray fittings to the brake backing plates, connect them to the hose connector with tubing, and install the hose connector almost anywhere you want on the trailer. After a day of boating, you simply hook up your garden hose to the connector and run the water to rinse away the salt residue.

Brake flush kits are available as options from trailer manufacturers or on the aftermarket. Installation is a not terribly difficult project for yourself or any competent trailer mechanic.

Tie-Downs

One of the last things you want while towing is to have the boat bouncing up and down or shifting on the trailer. To avoid this, you need good-quality straps at the bow and stern, and for the belt-and-suspenders personalities, possibly amidships as well.

Some boat trailers come with permanently mounted, retractable tie-down straps, but all trailerable boats and nearly all boat trailers at least provide places to secure loose straps. These provisions might be nothing more than a metal eye protruding from the transom, a well-placed trailer frame member, or a conveniently located hole in a trailer cross member, but you can always find appropriate places to lead, anchor, and secure a tie-down.

It may be tempting to save a few dollars on your tie-down gear and use a handy piece of rope. Don't! Use a dedicated, web-style strap with stout metal hooks at one or both ends and buckles or ratchet devices to put strong tension on the connection. Seatbelt-type ratcheting tie-downs are fast and easy to use and give you an absolutely taut and secure lashing.

Side-mounted, pivoting jack stands in the down and up positions.

Every boat trailer needs reliable tie-down straps to keep the boat secure on the road. (TRAILER BOATS)

Ratcheting tie-downs that are permanently installed on the trailer make securing the boat particularly easy. (BOATBUCKLE)

If you mount the strap permanently on the trailer, you don't have to search for tie-down straps in the boat and tow vehicle each time you load the boat. This makes boat retrieval fast and easy.

You can find tie-down straps at any boat dealer and just about any sporting goods outlet that carries trailer supplies. They are also abundantly available through the Internet. One leading brand is BoatBuckle, which comes in a range of configurations for lashing down your boat at the transom, the bow, or amidships.

5

The Art of Towing

Towing a trailer for the first time is intimidating. Anyone who tries to tell you differently has forgotten their first hours, when the heart seemed to stay in the throat and sweaty palms made gripping the steering wheel any tighter nearly impossible. After you gain experience and confidence, these tensions will disappear.

How quickly you master the art of towing a boat trailer depends on one very basic concept—learning the nuances of how your tow vehicle interacts with your boat trailer, and especially how they react as a unit. For example:

- What effect does your trailer have on your tow vehicle's acceleration, braking, and steering?
- What line do the trailer's wheels take as you round a corner?
- How do the tow vehicle and trailer react going over bumps and dips in the road or to a sudden gust of wind?
- How quickly does the trailer respond to changes in steering while you're backing up?
- How sharply can you turn before the trailer tongue puts a crease in your tow vehicle's rear bumper or bodywork?

Initially, this is anything but intuitive. With practice, however, you will develop a feel for all these things, and just like driving a vehicle without a tow, towing will *become* intuitive.

PRE-TOWING ROUTINE

Like a good pilot, a driver who plans to tow a trailer needs to have confidence that everything is in order before starting the engine. This involves using a systematic pre-towing routine every time you hook the trailer to the hitch. The more systematically you approach this task, the less likely you'll be to miss something.

There are three phases to the procedure: (1) check the tow vehicle, (2) check the trailer and boat, and (3) connect your tow vehicle to the trailer. This takes less than 10 minutes to complete, but it can eliminate the vast majority of trailer problems that occur on the highway.

Check the tire pressure on the tow vehicle and the trailer before hitching up.

Check the Tow Vehicle

This is a very basic check of your tow vehicle and shouldn't take long to finish. If you find anything wrong during this check, the safest course of action is to fix it before you set out. Here's the list:

- Check tires for tread wear. Slip a penny into the grooves, with Lincoln's head resting on the bottom of the middle tread groove. At its thinnest point, the tire should have at least enough tread to touch Lincoln's head.
- Be sure tires are inflated to the pressure indicated on the doorjamb or in the owner's manual. Do NOT inflate the tires to the pressure indicated on the sidewalls: this is the *maximum* pressure the tire can accept, not the *recommended* pressure for your tow vehicle.

These are the first things to check on your tow vehicle.

- Check fluid levels and look for any signs of leaking hoses.
- Check fan belt and battery cables for tight connections.
- Make sure the lights and turn signals are working properly.

Check the Trailer and Boat

Start the second phase at either end of the trailer. I like to begin at the stern of the boat and work my way toward the bow:

Tilt the engine to the full up position and lock or brace it in place before towing.

- Check that the transom (and bow) tie-down straps are tight and secure. These straps are very important in keeping the boat and trailer together while on the road. If you don't use them or leave them too loose, the boat will bounce around when the trailer hits rough pavement. This could result in damage to the hull from banging on the bunks or rollers.
- Place the outboard engine or outdrive in the full up position and lock it in place. If the outboard doesn't have a locking mechanism, use an engine lower-unit brace to keep it from bouncing around.

TRANSOM SAVERS

An engine support stand is a valuable accessory to use while towing an outboard-powered boat, especially if you tow over rough roads. The device slips between the lower unit of the outboard and the aft center roller of the trailer or the trailer's rearmost cross member, supporting some of the weight of the engine. These devices are commonly called *transom savers,* because the weight of the engine flexing back and forth on the transom can weaken or even break the transom.

There are a variety of transom savers to choose from at boat dealers, marine supply houses, and on the Internet. They include such brands such as Attwood, Swivl-Eze, and Springfield Marine. One I like is the T-Rex Transom Saver with Prop Lock, from DuraSafe Locks. This particular model has a built-in cushion that prevents wear on the lower unit. It also stabilizes the outboard during towing and deters theft of expensive props and the Transom Saver itself.

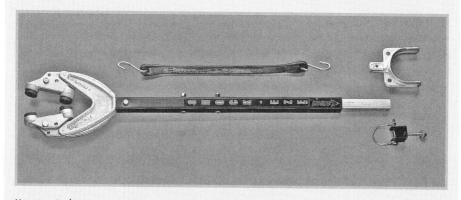

Use an engine brace or transom saver to support the lower unit of an outboard engine while towing. (SWIVL-EZE)

- Check the trailer tires for proper inflation (use the psi indicated on the sidewall) and condition. Underinflated tires overheat and are the leading cause of blowouts. Tires in poor or worn-out condition are a close second. Wiggle the wheels to make they are secure; bad wheel bearings and loose lug nuts are not something you want to deal with at 60 miles per hour (mph).
- Using a torque wrench, check the lug nuts against the trailer manufacturer's specifications. If they're loose, use a torque wrench, not an impact wrench, to tighten them. It is easy to overtighten lug nuts, which can become a real pain if you later find yourself on the side of the road trying to change a flat tire by hand.
- Inspect the trailer springs and hangers (the brackets to which the springs are attached) to make sure everything is tight and in proper working order. Broken axle springs and bent hangers will create severe handling problems and cause tire wear.

Make sure the bow is up against the bow stop and the winch strap and bow safety chain or tie-down straps are tight.

- Check that the winch strap is tight and the boat's bow is snugged up tight against the bow stop. Install and tighten the bow safety chain or tie-down straps.
- Make sure you have the proper safety gear inside the boat, including U.S. Coast Guard–approved personal flotation devices (PFDs) for each person on board, a throwable flotation device or cushion, fire extinguishers, a whistle or handheld horn, distress signals or flares, and whatever else the Coast Guard and local boating regulations require.
- Make sure all gear in the boat is *securely* stowed. Any heavy, loose items that are simply resting on the cockpit sole, such as full ice chests, anchors, gas cans, or batteries, can do a lot of damage if they go sliding around during hard acceleration or braking. Lightweight items such as clothing and boat cushions are almost certain to fly out of the boat while you're driving unless they're stowed inside a locker or in the cabin.
- Turn off all cooking and heating fuels on the boat at their source. For example, turn off propane at the tank, not just at the stove. This is state law in most places, as well as just common sense if you think about what could happen during a highway accident.

Making the Connection

After you've completed phases 1 and 2, it's time to hitch the trailer to the tow vehicle. Although this is a straightforward process, it involves a number of details, which if overlooked, could result in serious problems:

- Check that the hitch, drawbar, and trailer ball are the proper ones for the boat and trailer you are towing. The size of the required ball is stamped into the body of the trailer coupler: make sure this size matches the size stamped into the ball on the hitch's mount or drawbar. Most trailers for smaller boats have a coupler that takes a 2-inch-diameter ball; couplers for larger boat trailers usually take a $2^5/_{16}$-inch ball. Make sure the ball is in good condition and that the retaining nut is tight.
- Apply a thin coating of grease or a special ball lubricant to the hitch ball. This will extend the life of the tow ball, and it may also prevent annoying squeaks between the coupler and the ball while towing. (You don't need to do this each and every time; once every two months should suffice.)
- Crank the trailer tongue jack until the bottom of the coupler is 1 to 2 inches higher than the top of the tow ball on your tow vehicle. This height allows you to back your tow vehicle under the coupler without jamming the tow ball into it (and possibly damaging the braking mechanism or bending the tongue jack).

- Align your tow vehicle with the trailer. Very, very slowly, back the tow vehicle toward the trailer. Have your spotter use hand signals or verbal directions to guide you. Stop when the hitch ball is directly under the trailer coupler.
- If you don't have a spotter to direct you, alignment becomes a bit more complicated but can still be done. Here's how:

  1. Look in the rearview mirror (or over your right shoulder) and position your tow vehicle so the bow of the boat is aligned with the middle of the rear window—or if you're in a pickup, with the center of the tailgate.
  2. When you are about 8 feet away from the bow of the boat, stop, put the vehicle in park, and set the emergency brake. Go back to the trailer to confirm how far you have to back up and if the hitch ball is inline with the trailer coupler.
  3. Get back in your tow vehicle, make any necessary steering adjustments, and again very slowly ease the vehicle back another few feet.
  4. Stop and repeat as necessary until you have the trailer hitch ball positioned perfectly under the trailer coupler.
  5. The key is to avoid ramming the trailer coupler into the vehicle's bumper, tailgate, or rear hatch.
  6. If the boat trailer is light enough, it may be easier to move the trailer the last few inches on its tongue jack instead.

- Once the ball is directly under the coupler, lower the tongue jack until all the weight of the tongue is on the hitch.
- Close the latch by pushing down on the handle. Insert the locking pin into the small hole and through both the coupler body and the locked-down handle to prevent the latch from opening during transit. (Instead of a locking pin, you can use a bolt and nut or a padlock, which adds some

BACKING AND HITCHING AIDS

There are several backing aids to help you align the tow ball and coupler. One is a rearview video camera positioned in the rear of the tow vehicle and aimed at the trailer ball and vehicle bumper. The monitor, of course, is in the vehicle's cab. Many vehicle manufacturers offer these cameras as options, or you can purchase them from an aftermarket source, such as Rostra Precision Controls.

Other backing aids are less high-tech. The Valley Industries Magnetic Hitch Aligners are a pair of telescoping fiberglass sticks with strong magnets for bases and fluorescent plastic balls on top. By placing one unit on the hitch and the other on the trailer coupler, you can use the bright plastic balls to align the hitch ball and the coupler.

Another device is a metal V-shaped guide that bolts to the hitch just ahead of the ball. As the tow vehicle backs up the last few inches to the trailer, the guide forces the trailer coupler to position itself right over the hitch ball.

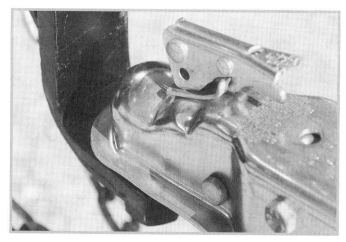

Here is a coupler latched onto the hitch ball. Note that the required safety pin has not yet been inserted through the hole in the latch lever.

Swing the tongue jack to the horizontal position and lock it in place.

degree of theft protection as well. Standard padlocks won't provide *much* security, however. If someone really wants your boat and trailer, they'll make short work of your standard, hardware-store lock with a standard, hardware-store bolt cutter. Special trailer locks that limit access to the shackle are available and will provide a greater measure of security.)

- Finish raising the jack all the way. If it's the pivoting type, swing it up and lock it in place. I have seen this latter step overlooked by a boater in a hurry to get going, resulting in a total wipeout of the trailer wheel jack assembly!

- If the trailer's wheels were chocked, remove the chocks and stow them securely in the boat. Do this now. You'll be amazed at how often you try to drive away with them still under the wheels. Ka-thump! (Many boatowners tie the bow chocks to the trailer using a short length of rope. This setup is handy when retrieving a boat on a steep ramp because it allows you to simply drive off the ramp without having to first remove the chocks. Just remember to pick them up and stow them as soon as you're off the ramp. You don't want them banging around at the end of their ropes as you tool down the highway!)

- Step back from the rig and observe it carefully from the side. Make sure the trailer sits parallel with the ground and in line with the chassis of the tow vehicle. If the tongue is too high or too low, your tongue weight may be off, and this will seriously affect trailer stability, tow vehicle steering, or both. (This is something that you should have confirmed previously; see Balancing the Load in Chapter 4.) However, if you find the balance is off, there are a few things you can check:

Is the boat properly snugged up against the trailer's bow stop?

Have you placed any unusual weight in the boat that might change the trailer's balance point?

Is the hitch ball at the wrong height? This will not only affect balance but also steering and stability. If it's too low, you might scrape the hitch on the ground as you drive across railroad tracks or through dips in the road.

If your tongue jack is not a pivoting type, make sure it's cranked up as far as it will go. (PETER DUPRE/AUTOWORD)

If your trailer still isn't sitting level, change the ball mount (shank) to one that places the hitch ball at the proper height, or use a hitch ball with a longer or shorter shaft.

This photo shows both correct and incorrect connection practices. Correct: The safety chains are installed properly—crossed and hooked into the loops from beneath. The S hook is oriented properly. Incorrect: The cable that actuates the brakes in case of a breakaway shouldn't be tangled in the chains and the latch lever has not been locked down.

- Attach the safety chains (or cables) by crossing them under the coupler and hooking them onto the hitch loops in the proper orientation. Hook the chain on the left side of the trailer to the loop on the right side of the hitch receiver, and vice versa. Crossing the safety chains provides a secure cradle should the trailer tongue pop loose from the ball: they'll hold the trailer tongue off the ground until you can come to a stop. If you don't cross the chains, the trailer tongue will drop onto the road surface, and it's unlikely you'll save either boat or trailer.

- Check the slack in the chains. You need to leave enough slack so the tow vehicle can pull the trailer around tight turns without tightening the chains. Too much slack, and the chains will drag on the ground, or they won't keep the trailer tongue off the pavement if they do come into play.

- Be sure you attach safety chains with a traditional open S hook such that the open part of the S faces the rear of the trailer. To do this, place the hook on the loop from underneath (see photo below). If you simply drop the hook over the top of the loop, it can easily bounce out while trailering. Some states now prohibit the use of open S hooks (without "keeper" tabs) and require the use of devices such as shackles or quick-links. Quick-links are special chain links with a barrel nut that unscrews to reveal a gap in the link. They take a few more seconds to apply than S hooks, but after you've slipped the link over the loop on the hitch and tightened up the barrel nut, there's no way it will come off accidentally.

Improperly attached safety chains. Although the chains are properly crossed, the S hooks have been merely dropped onto the loops from above, and they can easily bounce out. The latch lock pin is not in place, either.

- Attach the breakaway cable or chain (the one that applies the trailer brakes) from the trailer to the tow vehicle. Adjust the length so the brakes will engage if the trailer tongue falls onto the safety chains. Make sure there's enough slack so the tow rig can negotiate tight turns without putting tension on the

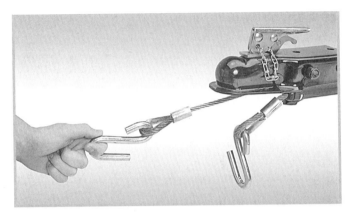

These safety cables are a nice alternative to chains. They're spring-loaded, so they can't bounce off of the hitch loop, and they're easily retracted to keep them out of the way when not in use. (TRACKER MARINE)

cable—you don't want it to apply the trailer brakes inadvertently. For much the same reason, don't wrap the breakaway cable around the safety chains. It's recommended that you attach the breakaway cable to the hitch itself. Avoid hooking it to the drawbar or around the ball (just in case the ball breaks off or the drawbar pulls out of the receiver).

- Make the electrical connection by inserting the plug on the trailer harness into the receptacle on the tow vehicle. Again, check for a sufficient, but not excessive, amount of slack.
- Check to make sure the taillights, side marker lights, and brake lights are working. Other drivers can't read your mind. If you are alone, turn each turn signal on and walk behind the trailer to make sure they are working properly. To check the brake lights when you're alone, position the trailer close to a wall and watch for the glow of the brake lights reflecting off the wall when you tap the pedal.
- With the tow vehicle and trailer in a straight line, adjust the mirrors so you can see the both stern corners of the boat. Adjust the passenger-side mirror down a little so you also get a glimpse of where the trailer's tires are on the road. You should also be able to see into the blind spot on the passenger side that is over your right shoulder, between the front passenger-side door and the bumper of the tow vehicle. (That's the area where other vehicles tend to be just when you want to make a lane change.) If you can't adjust the passenger mirror to see everything that you need to, you should add a special towing mirror.
- Do a complete run-though of your checklist to make sure you haven't missed anything.
- As soon as you begin to move the rig, and before you're in traffic, check the brakes. You should also be able to feel the trailer brakes engaging when you apply the tow vehicle's brakes. The feeling will be a momentary light jerk, and you'll feel the tow vehicle slow down with a little less nosedive than it does when there's no trailer behind.

lock pin secure   hitch pin in place and locked

trailer wiring   safety chains/   coupler latched
plug connected   cables attached

A proper and complete connection for a trailer with surge brakes with electric back-up disconnect.

SECURING THE BOAT TO THE TRAILER

Phase 1 of our checklist included the necessary step of strapping the boat securely to the trailer. This important step, which is frequently overlooked, is worth more attention.

Those new to boating often assume that attaching the winch strap to the bow eye and setting the anti-reverse lock on the winch is sufficient to keep the boat on the trailer. That's true around the boat ramp or the backyard, but not for the trip to the water or back home.

I'm reminded of a friend of mine who, when driving back from a boating trip in the Florida Keys, came upon a lot of flashing blue lights and a crowd of onlookers. As he passed the accident scene, he noticed the stern of a boat, complete with outboard engine, sticking out of a canopy of mangroves just off the highway—15 feet above the ground!

Here's what happened: The driver towing the boat had slammed on the brakes to avoid hitting a vehicle that had suddenly slowed down in front of him. Not able to slow quickly enough, the driver also swerved hard to his left in an attempt to avoid the impending rear-end collision. That didn't work either. When the two vehicles hit, the bow of the boat ran up over the bow stop, easily snapping the polypropylene winch rope clipped to the boat's bow eye. Like an Olympic long-jump skier going for the gold, the boat took flight into the woods, using the pickup's tailgate and cab as the launch ramp.

A boat coming loose from its trailer is not a pretty scene. I've witnessed the aftermath of several similar accidents: boats lying on the side of the road and off their trailers; sitting atop a crushed tailgate, with their bows embedded in a pickup cab; or mashed into the rear hatch of an SUV.

Flat-bottomed boats are the most prone to coming off bunk trailers. Their flat bottoms cannot be cradled in the V- or U-shaped arrangement of these trailers, which prevents side movement in V- and round-bottomed boats. Most

PRE-TOW CHECKLIST

Phase 1: Tow Vehicle Check

__ Tire treads OK
__ Tire pressure appropriate for towing
__ Hoses checked for leaks
__ Fan belt tight
__ Battery cable connections tight
__ Lights and turn signals working

Phase 2: Trailer Check

__ Transom straps tight
__ Outboard or outdrive up and locked
__ Trailer tire inflation and condition check
__ Lug nuts tight
__ Springs and hangers OK
__ Winch strap or cable tight; bow against stop; bow tie-downs tight
__ Safety gear secured in boat

Phase 3: Tow Vehicle and Trailer Connection

__ Hitch and ball sizes match
__ Ball tight and lubricated
__ Trailer set on hitch; coupler latched
__ Locking pin in coupler
__ Wheel chocks removed
__ Trailer and tow vehicle parallel and level
__ Safety chains correctly installed (crossed, with hooks aligned in proper direction)
__ Breakaway cable attached
__ Tongue jack up and locked
__ Electrical connection made and checked
__ Brakes checked
__ Mirrors adjusted

flat-bottomed boats also tend to be fairly light, so many owners seem to believe (erroneously) that their boats can be secured with a single rope.

That doesn't mean, however, that flat-bottomed hulls are the only candidates to become flying boats. Any hull type can become airborne if it's moving at 60 miles per hour and the trailer to which it's inadequately attached suddenly stops. Trailers with roller bunks are of special concern. Designed to make launching and retrieving a boat as easy as possible, rollers minimize the friction between the boat and the trailer, making any poorly secured hull ripe for flight.

Securing the Boat

You have several options when it comes to securing your boat to the trailer: winch straps or cables, bow-eye safety chains, bow tie-downs, and gunwale straps. We'll start with winch straps or cables because securing your boat to its trailer begins at the bow:

1. Position your boat so the bow is firmly against the bow stop roller or V. The bow eye must be below the roller or V.
2. Pass the winch strap or cable underneath the bow stop and between the winch supports.
3. Hook the winch strap or cable to the bow eye.
4. Tighten the strap or cable so that it pulls the bow forward and possibly down—never up.
5. Ensure that the winch uses a proper strap or cable—not a rope—and there is a hook on the end of it.

A properly secured boat bow. The boat's bow eye is below the trailer's bow stop. The bow is held down with a ratcheting tie-down strap, and the tie-down is backed up by the winch strap, which is pulling both forward and down. (BOATBUCKLE)

The winch strap, however, is just insurance. What should really hold the bow in place is a bow-eye safety chain or tie-down straps. A standard safety item found on many boat trailers, the bow-eye safety chain makes a superstrong connection between the bow eye and the winch or trailer frame, preventing the bow of the boat from moving forward, backward, sideways, or upward. It also takes some of the load off the winch as you motor down the road, increasing the winch's longevity.

If your trailer isn't equipped with a bow-eye safety chain, you can purchase one of a number of aftermarket bow tie-down straps that work in a similar fashion. These are typically adjustable, 3-foot-long, wide web-style straps with hooks on each end. In a pinch you can use any load securing strap as long as it can be suitably adjusted for length and has a high-enough load capacity to match or exceed those you'd find at marine dealers. *Never* use bungee cords or rope because they stretch and don't have the holding power, which defeats the purpose.

Gunwale straps go completely over the boat and hook to the trailer only at the ends. They can be difficult to keep snug because of their length, and they can mar a boat's finish where the webbing rubs against the boat during transit.

A better alternative is to use shorter tie-down straps, one on each side, running from gunwales to either the trailer frame or special eyes bolted or welded to the trailer frame specifically for this purpose. Attach the strap at the gunwale to a midships cleat or use a special strap with a gunwale hook.

There are advantages to using the shorter straps. They're more easily tightened and tend to stay tighter, plus there is less strapping in contact with the boat's gelcoat, reducing wear of the surface. But whether you use gunwale straps or the shorter side straps, it's a good idea to place a piece of cloth or soft pad between the strap and the gunwale surfaces to protect the gelcoat.

DRIVING THE RIG

The boat's now strapped securely on the trailer, and the trailer's hitched to the tow vehicle. It's time to start driving! Take your time. This is not a race.

Place stern tie-downs at both sides of the transom.

The best way to begin is to find a big, vacant parking lot or other open space where you can practice towing without the eyes of the world following your every move. But first, you have to get there! If you have never driven a trailer before, it might be wise to get a friend who's proficient in trailering to drive the rig there for you. This way your first towing experience won't be on narrow streets, amidst traffic. Your friend can also act as your spotter as you practice backing and turning maneuvers in the parking lot. If you're going solo, however, read this entire chapter carefully before taking the vehicle out on the road.

Spend the first hour or so in the parking lot just getting a feel of how your tow vehicle interacts with the trailer:

- Check the mirrors. If you can't see the boat trailer's wheels and the stern of the boat, readjust the mirrors so you can.
- Drive around slowly. Notice how the tow vehicle and the trailer react when you pull away from a stop and when you step lightly on the brake pedal.
- Make left- and right-hand turns. Make big, wide ones at first, then tighter ones as time goes on.
- Pay close attention to where the trailer wheels track in relation to the tow vehicle's front wheels. Knowing this relationship will help you avoid jumping curbs, hitting street signs, or dropping the trailer wheels off the pavement when you are making a turn.

To secure the boat to the trailer, you can use a single gunwale strap and extend it completely over the boat (top), or use two separate straps, one on each side of the boat (bottom). (BOATBUCKLE)

If you have the opportunity to practice with a trailer that has a different number of axles than yours, try it. Assuming that the loads are comparable, tandem-axle trailers put less strain on the rear of the tow vehicle than single-axle trailers. You'll notice that the tandem axle trailer feels a little more docile, not affecting the tow vehicle's acceleration or braking as much as a single-axle trailer.

You'll also notice right away that a single-axle trailer follows the tow vehicle's line more closely when making a turn, while a tandem-axle trailer's tires track further *inside* the line of the tow vehicle. The tighter the turn, the more they track inside.

BACKING

After you've gotten comfortable doing slow-speed maneuvers going forward, it's time to starting backing up. This is one of the few areas of towing where having a larger boat might be an advantage, since longer trailers are easier to control when backing than shorter ones.

Backing Straight

If the area you are using doesn't have marked parking spaces, place a half-dozen gallon milk jugs filled with water in a pattern that outlines a 10-foot-wide parking space or the entrance to a driveway or boat ramp. (You can also use traffic cones or any other objects that you can see easily and that won't cause any damage if you run over them.) Position the jugs 50 feet straight behind the boat trailer (which should be perfectly in line with the tow vehicle for your first attempts). The object is to back up *slowly* until the boat trailer is "parked" in the marked space.

Don't hurry. The slower you back a trailer, the easier it is to control. Place your hands at the 5 o'clock and 7 o'clock positions on the steering wheel. This hand positioning makes controlling a trailer while backing up the least taxing on your brain:

To make the trailer move to your left—move your left hand up.

To make the trailer move to your right—move your right hand up.

Simple, isn't it? Don't worry how it works; the less you dwell on the mechanics of backing up a trailer, the faster you'll learn the art.

Finally be sure to use the side mirrors to watch the trailer as you back up—don't try twisting your neck into a chiropractor's dream.

The trailer is going to make little side-to-side moves as you back, so you'll need to make tiny steering corrections the moment you notice the trailer start to move in either direction. This is normal. Go slow and all will be well.

If the trailer gets badly out of line, stop. Pull forward until the boat trailer is straight, and try again. Notice how quickly the trailer turns in relation to the vehicle speed and steering adjustments. There's always a bit of a time lag between the time you make the steering adjustment and the time that the trailer reacts.

Keep practicing and don't get nervous. You're not at a boat ramp holding up the show. It takes *everyone* some time to learn how to maneuver a 20- or 30-foot-long load in tight confines.

Turning While Backing

After you've learned how to make the trailer *not* turn while backing, it's time to learn how to make it turn in the direction you want it to go. Again, make it a game and take your time.

When you approach any parking space or boat ramp from the side, always give yourself as much room as possible. The closer the tow vehicle is to the ramp or parking spot, the tighter you must turn the tow vehicle to make the trailer turn sharper. This maneuver is definitely more difficult than making wide, gentle turns.

Determine the Jackknife Angle

Before you start the exercise, you want to first determine how sharp an angle you can put between your tow vehicle and trailer before you jackknife the rig and cause damage. If you have a friend helping, back slowly with the wheel turned in either direction while your friend watches the clearance and gives you the signal when to stop.

If you're practicing solo, go especially slowly. Close the angle a few degrees at a time, then stop the truck, get out, and take a look at the angle. Then get back into the truck and close the angle a few more degrees. Don't cut it too close. You want to leave yourself some room for error.

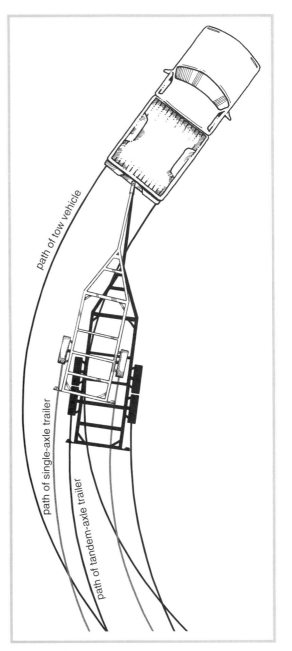

All trailers will track to the inside of a turn. The more axles the trailer has, the more the trailer will track to the inside of the turn.

(CHRISTOPHER HOYT)

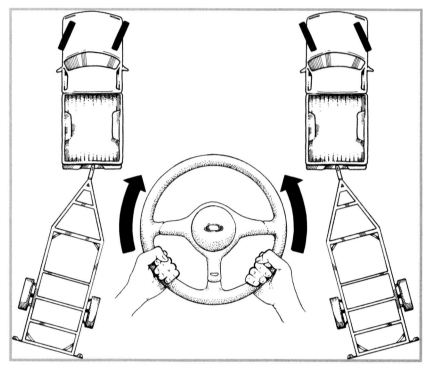

When you've found the minimum angle that you're comfortable with, sit in the driver's seat and carefully observe how the trailer and boat look in your side mirror. Remember that image—burn it into your brain—and make sure that the boat never looks any closer than that when you back up in the future. Repeat the process for the opposite direction.

To back a trailer, grip the wheel at the 5 o'clock and 7 o'clock positions. Raise your right hand to make the trailer go right; raise your left hand to make it go left. (*TRAILER BOATS*, DRAWN BY CHRISTOPHER HOYT)

Practice

Now we're ready to begin the exercise. Pretend you are on a narrow street, and you're trying to back the trailer into a driveway. Or imagine that you're at a small boat ramp where you can't pull forward far enough to straighten the trailer, and you have to approach the ramp from an angle. Here goes:

1. Make your first approach so the ramp comes up on your right, as this is the normal flow of traffic at a boat ramp.
2. With your rig perpendicular to the direction you plan to back, pull the trailer at least two boat lengths past the entrance to indicated by your markers.
3. Stop the tow vehicle and position your hands at 5 o'clock and 7 o'clock on the steering wheel.
4. Move your right hand upward to make the trailer turn toward the opening. Keep in mind the jackknife angle and how sharp the trailer can turn without hitting the tow vehicle.
5. Slowly ease the tow vehicle backward while also watching:

   • Where the right-side trailer tires are going
   • Where the front of your tow vehicle is in relation to other obstacles
   • The clearance between your tow vehicle and the trailer

6. If the trailer isn't turning fast enough, move your right hand up more. If it's turning too sharply, pull your right hand down a little.
7. When the rear of the trailer is just entering the opening, re-center the steering wheel to begin straightening the trailer so that it moves cleanly between the

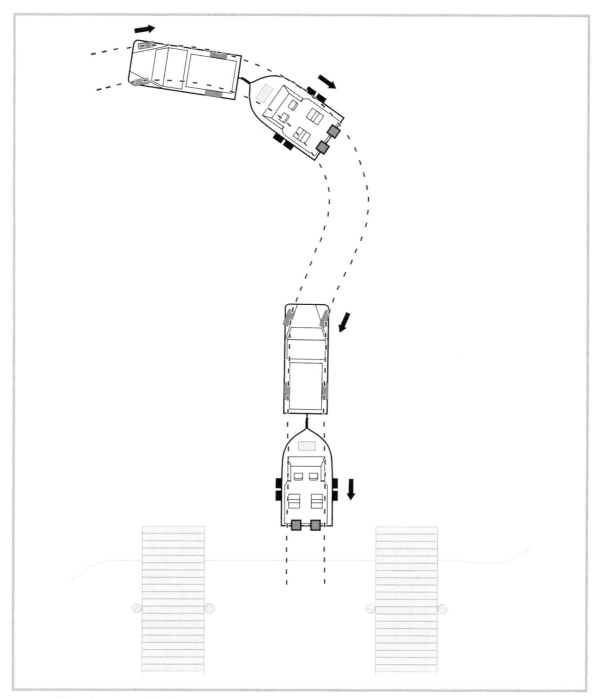

Give yourself as much room as possible when turning while backing. (PETER DUPRE/AUTOWORD)

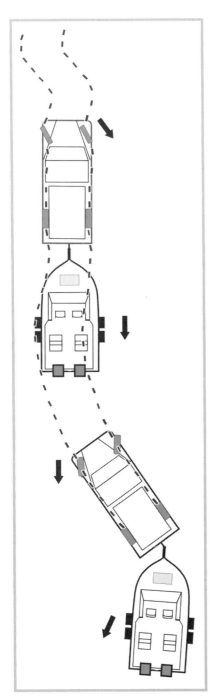

When backing, go slowly and try to make lots of small corrections rather than a few large ones.
(PETER DUPRE/AUTOWORD)

markers. It is a very common mistake to wait too long before beginning to straighten the trailer.

8. If just centering the wheel doesn't do the trick, counter-steer by raising your left hand a bit, then straightening out again.

9. Remember that it takes the trailer and tow vehicle a few feet of travel for steering corrections to take effect, so think ahead of the trailer.

Practice this angled backing maneuver again and again, changing the distance from the entrance at which you begin. When you can do it consistently and reliably in a variety of situations, begin working on turns to the left side. The procedure is the same.

THE TIGHT-S TURN

Along with the essentials of being able to back a trailer in a straight line and at a sharp angle, another very useful skill is the ability to align the boat trailer with the ramp entrance in as short a distance as possible. This saves time as well as the drama of backing a long distance.

I learned this one years ago, when I pulled into a narrow two-boat launch site with a very small maneuvering area at the head of the ramp. I didn't see any way to make the turnaround to get the boat's transom pointed toward the lake in such tight confines. But fortunately, I had a friend with me that day who was a seasoned boater, and he showed me a trick, which has been a time-saver ever since. He called this trailering maneuver the tight-S.

Basically the maneuver calls for you to drive your tow vehicle perpendicular and as close to the ramp entrance as possible and then make a tight-S turn the moment the nose of the tow vehicle passes the near side of the ramp entrance.

In this description, we'll assume that the ramp is to the right of your vehicle:

1. Pull up as shown in the illustration opposite.
2. As soon as your front wheels are even with the near edge of the ramp, cut your wheel to make a hard left turn.
3. Hold this sharp turn almost as if you were initiating a U-turn. (It's essential to know how sharply you can turn the tow vehicle without jackknifing the trailer.)
4. Instead of making the U-turn, make a very sharp turn back to your right the moment the ramp appears off to your left rear.
5. The two tight turns in opposite directions will almost magically straighten out the trailer behind your tow vehicle and align both with the launch ramp.

This maneuver requires less time and distance than it would take otherwise, reducing your backing distance to the water and making you look like a launch-ramp pro. It's even fun to do.

Learning these towing skills in a parking lot will take all of a couple hours, after which you can head out on the road. A half-dozen trips to the local boat ramp will hone your skills even further. If you feel intimidated about performing them in public, plan your first few visits to the boat ramp for mid-morning or mid-afternoon during the middle of the week. Traffic is generally lighter, other boaters tend to be in less of a rush, and there's less pressure to launch and park quickly.

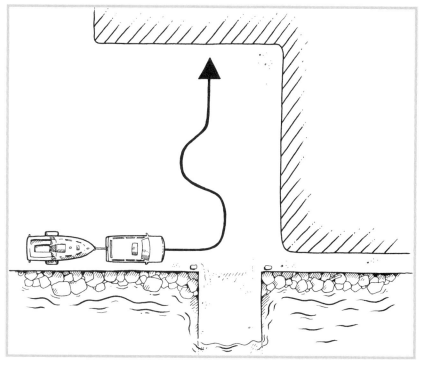

The tight-S turn gets your trailer lined up with the ramp when space is limited.
(CHRISTOPHER HOYT)

ON THE ROAD

After you've towed a few times, the little squeaks, rattles, and jerks that occur as you drive along become part of the ambience, and just like the noise from wind passing over the side mirrors, you won't even notice them. Beyond getting used to how your rig handles on the road are the mechanics and logistics of driving a vehicle with a trailer in tow, rather than just the vehicle.

Stopping and Starting

One aspect of towing that you must constantly be aware of is the dramatic difference in vehicle acceleration and stopping caused by the added weight of the boat and trailer. For example, a full-size, four-door pickup traveling 60 mph (88 feet per second) on dry pavement typically stops in about 150 feet in an emergency braking situation.

Add a 4,500-pound boat/trailer package to the equation and that distance jumps to 220 feet—a difference of 70 feet or 47 percent! If a vehicle stops suddenly in front of you, or a deer or a child enters the roadway, 70 feet will make a big difference in whether or not you can stop in time. Bear this in mind for other slowing and stopping situations, such as toll plazas and highway exits; all intersections (whether unregulated or controlled by stop/yield signs or traffic signals); school zones; residential areas; and wildlife-crossing areas.

As a guide to safe speeds, apply the 4-Second Towing Rule: under good road conditions, whatever your driving speed, leave at least 4 seconds between your vehicle and the one ahead of you. To do this, pick out a landmark on the highway fairly far ahead of you, such as a signpost, a tree, or a large rock. When the vehicle ahead of you reaches the landmark, count "one-thousand one, one-thousand

		Minimum Safe Following Distance (in feet)	
Speed (mph)	**Distance Traveled per Second (in feet)**	**Dry Pavement**	**Marginal Conditions**
25	37	148	222
35	52	208	312
45	66	264	396
55	81	324	486
60	88	352	528
65	96	384	576

Table 5.1 SAFE FOLLOWING DISTANCES WHEN TOWING

two, one-thousand three, one-thousand four." If your vehicle has not passed the landmark before the end of that count, you are following at what may be considered a safe distance. Any sooner and you are essentially tailgating, regardless of how far you appear to be from the other vehicle.

If the road conditions are the least bit compromised, say from light rain or dirt or gravel on the surface, then leave at least 6 seconds between your car and the one ahead of you.

Table 5-1 offers time-distance estimates for both the 4- and 6-second rules.

Acceleration is also affected by the additional weight of the boat and trailer. It takes almost twice as long for a vehicle towing a medium-sized boat to accelerate from 0 to 60 mph, or from 30 to 50 mph, as it does without a tow. Leave yourself plenty of space between vehicles when pulling into traffic from a side street, merging with highway traffic from an entrance ramp, and pulling into the opposite lane to pass.

Long-Distance Driving Checks

When you're on a long-distance trip, take every opportunity to stop and check your load. Tie-down straps can loosen, safety chains can come unhooked, tires can begin to wear unexpectedly, and wheel bearings can get overheated. Stop frequently at rest areas and use the pre-towing checklist to make sure that everything's still in good shape. Add to it a quick bearing check: kneel down and place your hand on the bearing caps. If they're warm, you're OK. If they're uncomfortably hot to the touch, you've got a serious problem, and you may have just avoided a disaster. Don't continue driving until you've diagnosed and repaired the problem.

City Driving

One of the driving environments that is unavoidable at some point in time is maneuvering through city traffic and congested streets. These are conditions that require undivided driver attention when there's a trailer in tow. In other words, stay off the cell phone, put down the map, and don't fiddle with the stereo or engage in any activity other than concentrating on driving. You constantly have to be thinking a full block or more ahead when towing a boat trailer; for example:

- Anticipate lane changes.
- Use your rearview and side mirrors, and look over your shoulders, to make sure there's no traffic in your vehicle's blind spots.
- Use turn signals long before making a turn or changing from one lane to another to warn the drivers around you.
- Stop on yellow lights instead of trying to beat the red.
- Swing wide on corners to avoid running the sharper-turning trailer's tires over curbs.
- Survey a parking lot before you pull in and find there's nowhere to park or no easy way out.
- Stay in the right-hand lane and drive at a safe speed.
- Take the safe route, even if it adds time to your trip.

Highway Driving

Highway driving is similar to city driving regarding thinking ahead, except that instead one block, you need to think a half-mile ahead. Your vehicle is twice as long and twice as heavy as usual. Therefore, every action will take twice as long to execute, twice as far to stop, and twice as long to get up to a certain speed.

Dips, bumps, and rough road surfaces have more effect on vehicle control when you are towing a trailer. A little dip in the road feels like a big dip. The effect of wind from passing trucks is magnified with a trailer in tow. Be prepared for the wind blast to hit, stay calm, make small steering corrections, and stay off the brakes.

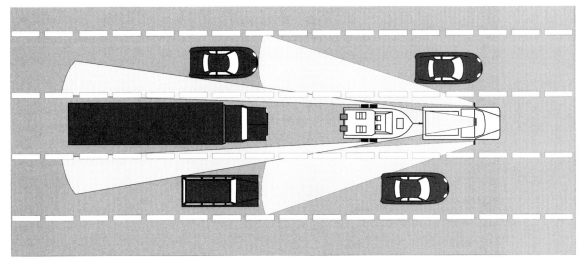

Anything that's not in or directly behind the light-shaded wedges is in your blind spot. Don't change lanes until you've looked over your shoulder
to see if another vehicle is lurking there. Depending on the height of your boat, vehicles directly behind you may be invisible as well.
(PETER DUPRE/AUTOWORD)

If you overtake a slower vehicle on a multilane road and wish to pass, turn on your turn signal, look in the mirrors, and look over both shoulders to check the mirrors' blind spots before moving into the passing lane. Pass as quickly as you can, but do not move back into the right lane until the vehicle you've just passed is well behind the trailer. It's great if the person you passed is courteous enough to flash their lights, letting you know it's safe to return to the slow lane, but this is a rarity and shouldn't be expected.

When towing a boat, it takes three to four times more distance to pass another vehicle. So when it comes to passing on a two-lane road—don't—unless you have a passing lane and/or *a lot* of distance to make the maneuver.

Bad Weather Driving

If you should get caught towing in snow or icy conditions, the safest thing to do is to pull off the road and wait until the road conditions improve. A boat trailer is the tail that wags the proverbial dog on slick surfaces—and the tail can wag instantly and with a lot of whipping force. This is also true in heavy rain or where there's standing water. Both conditions can result in hydroplaning, in which the tires plane over the surface of the water instead of staying in contact with the pavement, resulting in loss of traction. Obviously, this can instantly put the tow vehicle and trailer in an out-of-control situation.

Blowouts

Having a tire blow out is one of the most unnerving experiences that can occur when towing a trailer. Many drivers' first reactions are to lift off of the accelerator, hit the brakes, and quickly steer the vehicle to the side of the road. Wrong.

According to driving school experts such as Jeff Payne, President and CEO of Driver's Edge (a Las Vegas–based driving school sponsored by Bridgestone), if you experience a blowout, it doesn't make any difference what type of vehicle you are driving—the proper driving technique is always the same:

1. Keep a firm grip on the wheel. Do *not* slam on your brakes.
2. *Accelerate lightly* for an instant to preserve vehicle momentum (or at least maintain constant accelerator pedal pressure).
3. At the same time, steer gently away from the side of the flat to offset the pulling caused by the blown tire and to keep the vehicle in its lane.
4. Once you've stabilized your vehicle, turn on your four-way (hazard) flashers.
5. Brake slowly and lightly to slow down. Again, *do not slam on the brakes.*
6. Make your way carefully to the side of the road.
7. Reduce speed to 15 mph or less before leaving the pavement and pulling onto an unpaved shoulder.
8. Park your rig as far off to the side of the shoulder as possible to allow yourself room to change the blown tire without your backside hanging out in the travel lane.
9. Set out the emergency road triangles found in your vehicle safety kit (you do have one, right?) to warn other drivers that your vehicle is stopped.
10. Proceed to change the flat.

Towing Speed and Fuel Economy

Safety isn't the only good reason to slow down. Your wallet will appreciate it too. According to the Environmental Protection Agency (EPA), tests designed to imitate highway driving reveal that 54 percent of a tow vehicle's engine power is used to overcome aerodynamic drag. The faster you drive, the harder the engine has to work to push through the air, and the more fuel it consumes in doing so.

"The best fuel economy for the typical truck or SUV is cruising right around 40 miles per hour," explains Roger Clark, senior manager for General Motors' Energy Integration and Fuel Economy Learning Vehicles Program, which handles fuel economy development for all GM trucks and SUVs. "A good example of how drag affects fuel economy is a truck that has a 21 miles per gallon highway [pre-2008] EPA number. Drive at 10 miles per hour faster average speed, and drag causes that fuel economy to fall about 1.5 miles per gallon. Average 60 miles per hour and your mileage will drop another 1.5 miles per gallon. Run just above 70 miles per hour and your fuel economy is less than 14 miles per gallon instead of 21 miles per gallon."

As you can imagine, adding yet another component of drag to your vehicle in the form of a boat and trailer puts an even greater damper on fuel economy. When the gross weight of the trailer is more than half the weight of the tow vehicle, the added weight and surface area moving through the wind can easily reduce your tow vehicle's fuel economy by 40 percent. As trailer weight goes up, fuel economy drops even further.

TOWING ETIQUETTE

Towing etiquette and towing safety go hand in hand. You're not entitled to any special privileges just because you have

FUEL ECONOMY TIPS

Really want to eke out a little more fuel economy from your tow vehicle? Here are some suggestions from the experts at the EPA and the resulting benefits. As you'll see, it all adds up to quite a savings.

Drive smart. Aggressive driving (speeding, rapid acceleration and braking) wastes gas. It can lower your gas mileage by 33 percent at highway speeds and by 5 percent around town.

- Fuel economy benefit: 5 to 33 percent
- Equivalent gasoline savings: $0.15–$.95/gallon (based on $3/gallon)

Slow down. Gas mileage decreases rapidly at speeds above 60 mph because the vehicle pushes more wind. Each 5 mph you drive over 60 mph is like paying an additional $0.20 per gallon—or more—for gas.

- Fuel economy benefit: 7 to 23 percent
- Equivalent gasoline savings: $0.17–$0.67/gallon

Breathe easy. Replacing a clogged air filter helps ensure the proper fuel-air mixture for optimum combustion efficiency and reduces the energy the engine must expend pumping air.

- Fuel economy benefit: up to 10 percent
- Equivalent gasoline savings: up to $0.29/gallon

Stay tuned. Fixing an engine that is noticeably out of tune or has failed an emissions test can improve its gas mileage by an average of 4.1 percent, though results vary based on the kind of repair and how well it is done. If your car has a faulty oxygen sensor, your gas mileage may improve as much as 40 percent.

- Fuel economy benefit: 4 to 40 percent
- Equivalent gasoline savings: $0.12–$1.16/gallon

Air up. You can improve your gas mileage by keeping your vehicle's tires inflated to the proper pressure. Underinflated tires can lower gas mileage by 0.4 percent for every 1 psi drop in pressure of all four tires. Properly inflated tires are safer and last longer.

- Fuel economy benefit: up to 3 percent
- Equivalent gasoline savings: up to $0.09/gallon

Want to find out how much your annual fuel bill is going to be for the vehicle you're driving? The U.S. Department of Energy maintains a cool fuel cost calculator on the Internet: www.fueleconomy.gov/feg/savemoney.shtml.

an expensive toy behind your truck. Since your braking performance and acceleration are reduced, it's only simple courtesy to avoid impeding the normal flow of traffic. Rather than pulling out in front of other drivers and then moving away so slowly that they have to stomp on the brakes, wait for a clear opening—one that's a bit longer than you would need without a trailer on the hitch.

Before pulling into the opposite lane to pass another vehicle, remember that it will take you much longer to accelerate to passing speed. If other vehicles behind you are also waiting to pass, your slower performance may mean they lose their chance.

Tailgating, even if it weren't dangerous and illegal, is just plain discourteous and generally counterproductive anyway. Making the driver in front of you nervous will probably not make him drive faster—in fact, it might slow him down.

It is a courtesy, not to mention lawful, to have the trailer lights connected and functional. Nothing is more annoying to boaters and non-boaters alike than a person who expects those around them to read their minds regarding their intent to brake, turn, or change lanes. Check out who's behind and beside you before changing lanes, and use your directional signals before making your move.

Etiquette also plays a role when you enter a gas station or restaurant parking lot, or stop by the mall to get those last-minute provisions before you hit the water. I learned this aspect of boating etiquette as a member of a bass club, when we would travel to event locations in convoys of ten to twenty vehicles, each with a boat in tow. One of my boating mentors in the club made it a point to park in the farthest reaches of parking lots away from store or restaurant entrances. This practice avoids taking up two or more of the coveted parking spaces near the entrance, and at the same time, it almost always ensures you won't be blocked into your parking space by other parked cars whose drivers don't understand how much space a trailer needs to turn and maneuver.

At gas stations, the best pump to shoot for is the one on the outside of the island that allows you to pull straight through to exit the area. Avoid blocking access to another pump or obstructing the drive-through lane beside the pumping area. Failing to do so will earn you nasty stares.

6

Launching and Retrieving Your Boat

What happens on the launch ramp justifies everything from purchasing and outfitting your tow vehicle and trailer to learning how to drive the rig. If you can't get the boat trailer backed down the ramp and the boat smoothly in the water, it doesn't matter how well you drive, how great a tow vehicle you have, how fancy the boat and trailer, or how well you have it all equipped. The same goes for the retrieval process.

There are two keys to success: having a system and practice. There are so many details to remember in launching and retrieving that you're bound to forget some, or be forced to do them in an inefficient order—unless, of course, you have a plan. And like almost any other procedure that requires skill and technique, the only way to get good at it is through repetition.

If you practice and hone your launching and retrieving routines on quiet weekdays, you'll have the confidence and techniques to launch and retrieve smoothly and efficiently on your first busy weekend. (You know, when fellow boaters are looking on critically while anxiously waiting for their turns on the ramp.)

THE LAUNCH RAMP

On your first visit to any boat launch, take some time to inspect the ramp and its surroundings before you back the trailer down the ramp. Park the rig where it is out of the way of others, get out, and take a look around. Examine the situation for the following factors:

- What is the approach to the ramp? Is there enough room to make a simple U-turn and back up, or are there restrictions or obstructions to your approach? If so, be prepared to do the tight-S maneuver described in the previous chapter. It seems that most boat launches are arranged so that ramp traffic approaches in a counterclockwise manner. The ramp comes up on your right, and you must execute a left turn as you pull your tow vehicle forward and present the rear of the trailer toward the ramp.
- Is the launch area constricted so that you will have to back onto the ramp at an angle? If yes, try to arrange it so that you back your truck to the right and the trailer to the left. This way, you'll be able to see the trailer out of your driver's side window.

Backing the trailer to the left is easier than to the right, because you can see the trailer from your driver's side window. (TRAILER BOATS)

• How many lanes are there? Some ramps are strictly one-vehicle-at-a-time setups. Others can accommodate two, three, or more boats simultaneously. On multilane ramps, the choice of lane is often influenced by how comfortable you are backing a trailer in crowds. Most first-timers choose the outer lanes, since they can only get in their neighbors' way on one side. (Of course, you still have to pay attention not to strike inanimate objects on the other side.) Those with more experience usually choose whichever lane looks like it's going to be faster. More often than not, especially at busy boat ramps, courtesy calls for you to wait in line until the next available lane is open. Even when no one else is around, make it a practice to choose one side of the ramp or the other. This way, if someone arrives to launch their boat, they'll have an open lane.

• What are the width of the lanes? Lanes that are 16 feet wide are more forgiving than narrower 12-footers. If you're dead center in a 12-foot-wide ramp, you have 2 feet on each side of an 8-foot-wide boat—just enough to move all around the rig comfortably. If you're just 1 foot off center, it may be difficult or impossible to work on the tight side.

• What is the ramp made of? Poured, textured concrete? Gravel? Mud? Even if it's a good solid surface, is it clean? Is it covered with mud or slippery algae below the surface of the water? Will you be able to pull the boat out of the water on a slippery surface, especially if your tow vehicle does not have four-wheel drive? Be careful walking on ramps made from precast concrete slabs with gaps in between. These often make good driving surfaces, but they are also notorious ankle-twisters.

• How steep is the ramp? Ramps shallower than a 12 percent slope may

On multilane boat ramps, choose one lane and stay in it. The other lanes may be quiet when you begin, but someone else might show up and want to use the ramp too.

force you to back your trailer and tow vehicle farther into the water than you might wish. Ramps steeper than 15 percent can be difficult to pull a loaded trailer up, unless traction is excellent.

- Does the driving surface extend far enough into the water, or does it drop off abruptly? If the water is too murky to see the bottom, wait and watch as other boaters launch their boats. Do their trailers suddenly lurch down at some point? If so, how far? If there is a big

When dealing with narrow ramps, try to place the trailer dead center on the ramp to give yourself room to work all the way around. (PETER DUPRE/AUTOWORD)

drop-off, pay careful attention to where it is, and make sure you don't back your trailer wheels into it. Backing off the end of a boat ramp can damage the trailer and create problems trying to pull back out of the water. For insurance, have someone spot you when you're backing up.

- Is there a dock or pier to which you can tie the boat as soon as it comes off the trailer? If not, is there a soft beach nearby where you can board passengers and where the boat can sit while you park the truck and trailer? If neither of these are present, you'll have to think carefully about the logistics of getting the boat afloat, parking the rig, and getting everyone on board.
- Is the wind blowing? Current flowing? Which direction? If you have a choice of which side of a dock to launch on, choose the side that is

A poured concrete boat ramp. (This boater is taking up more than his fair share of this two-lane ramp, preventing anyone else from using it at the same time. Let's hope he's quick!)

Concrete-slab ramps make good driving surfaces but can be real ankle-busters. (LUND BOATS)

upwind or upcurrent, so that when the boat floats off the trailer, it will naturally drift to the dock.

• Where will you park? What are the hours of the parking area? Can you stay there as long as you plan to be boating?

If in doubt about these questions, ask other boaters at the boat launch. Most boat-ramp users are regulars and know all the hidden problems. Most will be friendly and willing to lend a hand.

PREPARING TO LAUNCH

Although you've scoped the ramp, you are still far from ready to launch. Before you back onto the ramp, pull into a parking space or the launch site's staging area and prepare the boat and trailer. If you don't, you'll likely forget something (maybe something important to safety), and you will certainly take too much time on the ramp, delaying someone else's turn.

If you've been driving at highway speeds for a long time, your trailer wheel bearings may be hot. If you submerge them in cold water while hot, they might warp or crack. This doesn't happen often, but it's a possibility. Additionally, any hot air inside the bearing cups will contract when the hubs hit the cold water, creating a vacuum and possibly pulling water into the bearings. (This is much less likely if you have bearing protectors.)

When backing down a steep ramp, you may temporarily lose sight of your boat. Having a spotter is a big help. (*TRAILER BOATS*)

Waiting a few minutes for your bearings to cool will not be wasted time, since you can use it productively for your pre-launch preparations:

- If your trailer has bearing protectors, check the grease or fluid levels and, if necessary, give them a shot of grease or oil to bring them back to proper level.
- If your boat has a cover, remove and stow it in the tow vehicle.
- Remove or retract the tie-down straps at the stern, on the gunwales, and at the bow.
- If your straps not retractable, remove and stow them in your tow vehicle—don't leave them hanging from the trailer frame. During the launch, the winch cable will be all that holds the boat in place, unless you've left the bow tie-down strap in place.
- Make sure the drain plug, located at the lowest point on the transom, is in place and secure. You can't imagine how many times I've seen boaters who were in a hurry to begin fishing or skiing launch their boats without checking the drain plug, only to have their boats sink at the launch ramp dock or their bilges fill up with water before they even got underway. Ramp watchers find such things quite humorous and a topic of conversation for months to come. But it's not that funny to the person sitting at the helm of the boat yelling for the tow vehicle driver to get the sinking boat back on the trailer.
- Secure the winch if you won't be using it. Most launching situations do not require the use of a winch, and most winches have a good locking mechanism that prevents the boat from accidentally sliding off the trailer. Still, if you have a manual

UNIMPROVED LAUNCH RAMPS

Several of the places where I've lived have given me the opportunity to launch boats in areas where paved boat ramps and wooden docks weren't even someone's dream. We're talking about launching a boat at ramps that were so unimproved they were nothing but a clearing just big enough to back a trailer into the water. Then once in, you were on your own.

An unimproved boat ramp, consisting of gravel or dirt, can make for difficult launching. Four-wheel drive is virtually a necessity.

I remember one situation quite well. I was with a couple of buddies who had the good fortune of receiving permission from a Mississippi land baron to go duck hunting on some of his prime river-bottom property. The Mississippi was flooded at the time, so to get out into the main river, we had to launch our 16-foot jonboat in a flooded field.

Fortunately, at that time I was driving a half-ton, four-wheel-drive Chevy pickup with good mud tires and a big Warn winch on the front bumper. I slipped the truck into four-wheel drive and eased the trailer off the gravel farm road and down a grassy, muddy slope in the field. The grass was all that saved me from having to use the winch to get back up out of the water.

When we returned to the truck some ten hours later, the water level had fallen nearly a foot, which required backing the truck and trailer even farther into the field.

On other occasions, I've launched and retrieved drift boats from river gravel bars, or into lakes where the boat ramps were nothing more than dirt or the natural gravel and rock smoothed from the trailer tires of hundreds or thousands of other boaters before me. I've even had to park my SUV a couple times and use an ATV to get a boat launched into farm ponds and flooded fields to fish and duck hunt. (Oh well, you do what you have to do.)

The keys to making the best of these situations is (1) study the ground before you begin backing up the trailer, and (2) rely on four-wheel drive to provide traction.

Don't forget to insert the drain plug before launching!

winch with a removable handle, it's a good safety measure to remove the handle and stow it in the tow vehicle. If someone accidentally unlocks the winch so it's in a free-spool mode, and the boat suddenly slides off the trailer with the winch cable still attached, the handle will spin rapidly, with enough force to break a wrist.

- On the other hand, it's also a good idea to leave the winch operational. Then, if for some reason, the boat needs to be winched back on the trailer immediately after it floats free, say the engine suddenly quits, you can quickly attach the winch strap or cable to the bow eye and crank it back onto the trailer. Later in the chapter, we'll look at various situations where the winch may or may not be used.

- If you have an outboard engine, remove the transom saver or engine support by tilting the engine up.

- Check the tilt mechanism, then leave the engine or sterndrive in the up position for the launch.

- Once again, make sure you install the boat's drain plug. It is amazing how frequently this obviously essential task is forgotten.

- Establish specific storage routines for tie-down straps, winch handles, boat covers, transom savers, and anything else that comes off the boat. Then make sure that you and anyone helping you follow these routines. There's no reason for anyone to be searching around for the winch handle when it's time to retrieve the boat. You *know* you are going to need it, so why not put it where you can find it easily?

- Load the boat now—not when it's on the ramp or in the water tied up to the dock. Dock space at most ramps is prime real estate designed for loading and unloading people, not gear. Load up all the gear you brought for your outing: personal flotation devices (PFDs), emergency radio, charts, first-aid kit, ice chests, fishing gear, water toys, sunblock, sunglasses, extra clothes, music, food, and water. Take your time stowing everything so items are secured and out of the way of the boat operator and passengers.

- If the light is low (e.g., it's dawn or approaching sunset) and your boat has removable running lights, mount them now.

- Check the operation of lights and other electrical and electronic equipment.

- Get docklines ready by attaching them to the bow and gunwale cleats on the side of the boat that will be against the dock after it is launched.

- Hang fenders on the same side of the boat.

- Stow away any lines you won't be using for the launch so they won't come free and trail in the water.

- If your boat has a stern-drive or inboard engine, open the engine cover and run the engine compartment blower. If it has an outboard engine, pump the fuel-line primer bulb until it's firm to ensure the engine has a good source of fuel right away.
- If you're going to power off of the trailer, have the boat operator get seated at the helm. As required by law, or your personal inclination, this is the time to have the skipper and passengers don and secure their PFDs.

Load the boat before pulling onto the ramp.

Once you have established that (1) the gear is aboard and stowed, (2) the docklines and fenders are ready, (3) all lights and electrics are working properly, and (4) the operator and passengers are set, it's time to head for the launch ramp.

Special Considerations for Trailer Lights and Brakes

As a precaution, it's a good idea to avoid submerging working, connected trailer lights in the water, as cold water can be sucked into the lamp assembly as the hot air inside cools and contracts. This could lead to cracking the hot bulbs or their filaments. How to deal with this depends upon the nature of your trailer's braking system.

Electric Braking System

If the surface of the ramp is dry, the slope is gentle, and the tow vehicle has good strong brakes, you can disconnect the trailer from the electrical harness before backing down the ramp. This way, the trailer lights won't be illuminated and the bulbs won't crack. However, the trailer brakes also will not work, which is why the conditions above must be in place.

Rig docklines and fenders before descending the ramp.

SAILBOAT PREPARATIONS

Besides all of the considerations that apply to powerboats, sailboats have their own specific preparations for launching.

TRAILERING

Before trailering a sailboat with a centerboard, swing keel, or lifting keel, it's a good idea to lower the appendage so that it rests on a cross member of the trailer while you drive. At the least, this will save wear and tear on the lifting pendant. In the case of a heavy lifting or swing keel, it may even prevent severe hull damage when the trailer runs over a large bump or hits a bad pothole.

Step sailboat masts in the parking lot before launching; however, make sure there are no overhead obstructions between the boat and the ramp.

RIGGING

If at all possible, it is best to rig your sailboat while it is still on the trailer. This applies to all but the smallest sailboats. Raising the mast can be difficult under the best of circumstances, and trying to do it while the boat is afloat, tipping this way and that, can be a recipe for frustration, if not disaster.

But before you step the mast in the boat launch's parking lot, take a careful look around for obstructions. Look for tree limbs that can get in your way, and overhead electrical wires that can cause electrocution if you run into them with an aluminum mast. If there are obstructions, you may have to choose between rigging the boat on the ramp itself, waiting until after you're afloat at a nearby dock, or beaching the boat near the ramp and doing it with the boat aground. However, if it's a busy day at the boat launch, think twice before committing to rigging on the ramp—anyone who monopolizes the ramp for a half hour will be subject to considerable disapproval.

PREPARING TO LAUNCH

Lift the centerboard or keel fully into the raised position so that it will clear the trailer frame. If the rudder is a kick-up type, hang it on the transom, since this is easier to do on dry land. Make sure it's in the raised position before you splash. If the rudder does not kick up, it may be too deep to be safely launched, and you may have to attach it when the boat is in the water.

See Chapter 7 for more details on sailboat launching.

If the ramp is steep or slippery, you might need those brakes. In that case, leave the connection intact.

Surge Braking System

As discussed in Chapter 4, surge brakes apply themselves when the trailer is pushed forward against the coupler attached to the tow ball. Consequently, some trailer's brakes engage when backing up because the tow vehicle is pushing the coupler against the brake cylinder just as if the tow vehicle is trying to stop. Every time you try to back up—especially on rough

Whether or not you disconnect the electrical connection between the tow vehicle and the trailer before launching may depend upon the type of brakes on your trailer.

ground or up the slightest of grades—the trailer brakes come on.

Most modern surge brakes avoid this in one of two ways. *Free-backing* brakes have a lockout mechanism in each wheel brake assembly that disengages the brakes when the wheels turn in reverse. Since there is no electrical connection between the tow vehicle and the brakes, you can electrically disconnect the trailer from the tow vehicle, thus protecting the trailer lights with no effect on braking.

Other surge braking systems use an electric solenoid in the coupler, which, when activated by the tow vehicle's backup lights and reverse gear, disengages the brakes (see Chapter 4).

Disconnecting the electrical connection between the tow vehicle and the trailer will disable the reverse-backing solenoid, so moving the tow vehicle in reverse may well activate the trailer brakes. If this is the case, you may have to leave the electrical harness connection intact or wait until you've angled the trailer downhill before disconnecting the trailer wiring connector from the tow vehicle. Make sure the tow vehicle is in "park" and the emergency brake is set before exiting the vehicle to unplug the trailer wiring connection.

If you do disconnect the electrical connection prior to launching, secure the pigtail of the tow vehicle's wiring harness so that it doesn't drag on the ground.

Light Board

One way to avoid the whole problem, regardless of the type of braking system, is to use a *light board* instead of standard trailer-mounted lights. This is simply a piece of 2 × 4 lumber, or similar, to which you attach the trailer's rear lights. Use a regular four-pin connector to make the electrical connection between the trailer's wiring and the board, and clamp the board to the boat's transom for travel. At the boat ramp and before launching, disconnect, unclamp, and stow the light board. This keeps the lights entirely out of the water.

Because light boards tend to be—shall we say—unlovely, one usually finds them restricted to older trailers. However, if you have a trailer with trouble-prone lights, a light board may be a good solution for you. In addition to avoiding the thermal shock problem with the bulbs, it keeps water out of the bulb sockets, reducing corrosion—another major cause of trailer light failures.

THE LAUNCH

For your first few outings, it is a good idea to have someone spotting you as you back onto the ramp. Some ramps angle down rather abruptly from the flat drive-in area, so that you may momentarily lose sight of both the boat and the ramp itself in your mirrors as you back up. If you don't have a friend or family member to act as your spotter, don't be shy about asking an experienced boater at the ramp to give you a hand. Most will be glad to oblige—especially if they're next in line and waiting for you to launch.

Work out a system of hand signals with your spotter and operator, as it is often difficult to hear shouted commands. Establish hand signals for basic instructions:

- Come back.
- Stop: Crossed arms or crossed wrists are a common signal for the tow vehicle driver to stop immediately.
- Go forward.
- Go left or go right: For clarity, "go left" and "go right" signals should actually mean "the back of the trailer needs to go this way/that way," rather than using named directions or directing how the tow vehicle needs to be pointed.

For example, if the back of the trailer needs to go to the tow vehicle driver's left, the person directing from the outside uses a full arm extension pointing to their left as they face the tow vehicle (up the ramp.)

Launching with Spotter, Boat Operator, and Driver

For this scenario, let's assume you have a full crew (i.e., boat operator, spotter, and you as the tow vehicle driver). Your boat operator is seated at the helm, the spotter is standing off to the side, and you are in the driver's seat of your tow vehicle. Here we go:

1. The spotter stands on the left (driver's) side of the rig, visible in your side-view mirror, but far enough back so that she can see exactly where the trailer's wheels are going as well as any obstructions and hazards.
2. As you back the vehicle, the spotter constantly moves position to retain a good view of the situation and to always have your face visible in the side-view mirror. If the spotter can't see you in the mirror, you can't see the spotter!
3. Watching the spotter's signals, back the trailer to the water's edge, then stop, keeping your foot on the brakes.
4. Have the spotter remove the bow strap, then move away from the trailer.
5. Back up slowly as the trailer wheels approach the water's edge, watch the boat operator for a signal when to stop. In most cases, the boat operator will want to start the engine as soon as the transom touches the water and the prop is submerged.

6. After the boat operator starts the engine and gives a thumbs-up, continue backing the trailer into the water until the stern floats free. Usually, the trailer is positioned correctly for launching when the water is just over the top of the trailer wheels or, at most, just above the fenders. There's no need to submerge the trailer any deeper. If the boat isn't floating free by that time, there's a problem. (For example, did you unhook the transom tie-downs?)

To avoid blocking the adjacent lane, try to do a better job keeping the tow vehicle and trailer straight on the ramp than this driver did.

7. Once the operator warms up the engine, the boat can be backed free from the trailer.

8. When the boat is clear of the trailer, pull the tow vehicle forward up the ramp and into the designated parking area.

Launching with Boat Operator and Driver

If it's just the boat operator and you, back down the ramp slowly, watching the tow vehicle mirrors to see where the trailer's tires are in relation to the ramp and any obstacles along the sides. Keep the boat and trailer parallel with the ramp. In other words, back straight down the ramp. (It is inconsiderate to block an adjacent lane.) If the ramp is wide enough, try to position the trailer so that it is 3 to 4 feet from the sides of the ramp or dock. This allows a little working room for the boat operator when the boat floats free of the trailer, but it is not so far away as to make it difficult to pull the boat to the dock using a dockline.

Backing into the water and releasing the boat use the same steps here as in the section above. However, either you or the boat operator will be the one releasing the boat not your spotter. If it's you that means you'll have to exit the truck. It's imperative that you place the vehicle in park and set the emergency brake to secure the vehicle on the slope. In fact, no matter the reason, while on the ramp, be sure to secure the vehicle whenever you have to leave it. This means standing on the parking brake and making sure the tow vehicle isn't going to roll backward.

Launching Solo

If you are doing the launching (and later the retrieving) alone, you have to be both tow vehicle driver and boat operator. More than ever, having a good system

After the boat operator has lowered the engine, the driver can unhook the bow strap and shove the boat off the trailer. (LUND BOATS)

is essential to doing it efficiently. A key element of the procedure is a long, strong dockline. We'll assume in this scenario that there is a dock adjacent to the ramp.

1. Tie a 50-foot length of $1/2$-inch dockline to the bow eye, or to a forward bow cleat on the side *opposite* the dock. Coil up the balance and place it in the bed of your pickup or the rear of your SUV (with the gate open).
2. Back the trailer down the ramp until the prop is immersed.
3. Stop the vehicle, make sure it's secure (park, emergency brake and chocks) on the slope, and get out.
4. Take the loose end of the bow line and secure it to a cleat, piling, or other strong tie-off point about a third of the way from the shore end of the dock. When the boat comes off the trailer, this line will prevent it from floating away.
5. If you have a trailer with roller bunks, unhook the boat once the stern is in the water and you can reach the bow eye without getting wet.
6. If your boat is on bunks and won't slide off the trailer by itself, unhook the winch strap from the bow eye.
7. Get back in the truck and back the trailer into the water until you see the boat float free of the bunks.

When launching alone, be prepared to push the boat off the trailer and immediately tie it up to an adjacent dock.

8. Get out of the tow vehicle (securing it again on the slope), walk down the dock to the dockline and pull the boat up to the dock. Or if you have friends or family waiting dockside, enlist their help to hold the dockline. When the boat slides off the trailer, they can pull it to the dock and secure it while you park the rig.

You'll note that as you do step 7, you'll be turning the boat around end-for-end. So if the dock is to the left of the boat ramp (as you face the water from the land), tie the dockline to a cleat on the boat's port (left) bow. That way, it'll be on the side nearest the dock after the boat swings around.

Another option is to tie the line to a stern cleat on the side nearest the dock. This will mean you'll be pulling the boat backward, a bit more difficult, but you won't be swinging it end-for-end, which requires more space.

If the ramp is busy, I back the trailer the last few feet into the water with a little momentum, hitting the brakes just as the boat floats free so that its momentum sends the boat drifting off the trailer and away from the ramp, instead of it just floating idly. (Be sure the line is secured at both ends.) The boat floats until the dockline tightens and pulls the boat back toward the dock. Then I quickly park the tow vehicle and trailer and run back to the ramp. This gets the truck out of the way a minute or two sooner, allowing the next guy to get ready to launch. This is a nice technique, but a lot can go wrong; don't try it until you have the basic launching routine down pat.

THE IMPORTANCE OF A DOCKLINE

It's dicey to try to hold the boat with your hand as it comes off the trailer. If you try doing so on a bigger boat, what usually happens is (1) you lose your grip on the boat and it floats away, or (2) you keep your grip on the boat, you lose your balance, and you fall into the water. The motto here: Always use docklines during the launching process.

It's better to use docklines, not your arms, to control the boat as it floats off the trailer.

Parking is often at a premium at boat launches. Park within the marked lines. (PETER DUPRE/AUTOWORD)

Parking

When the boat is clear of the trailer, slowly pull back up the ramp and into the designated trailer/tow vehicle parking area. If possible, find a parking spot that allows you to exit by pulling forward in order to circle back to the ramp when it comes time to retrieve the boat. Pull your tow vehicle as far forward as you can in the double-length parking spot so the trailer is clear of others making their way to a parking space. Park the tow vehicle and trailer so neither is straddling the lines. This is common courtesy to your fellow boaters.

Spaces on the end of parking rows are the easiest to use. Try to avoid middle parking places until you're comfortable maneuvering in tight quarters. The farther away from the ramp you park, the more room you'll have to maneuver when it comes time to retrieve the boat.

If other members of your party have vehicles, they should park in the areas with single-car-length spaces designated for just that purpose. The long parking spaces are only for vehicles with boat trailers. Again, this is a courtesy to fellow boaters—on busy days, trailer parking spaces are at a premium.

Take the keys, make sure nothing is left in the pickup bed or on the trailer, and lock the vehicle. Put the keys in a zippered pocket. If you are both the owner of the tow vehicle and the boat operator, keep the keys with you. If you don't own the tow vehicle, hand the owner his keys *after* you get in the boat. Don't toss him the keys while you are still on the ramp or dock! That's a great way to go swimming for keys.

Alternate Scenarios

You want to back the trailer only as far as it is necessary to get the boat floated off the trailer bunks. In practice, this distance depends upon the situation. Probably the most common scenario involves fully immersing the trailer wheels so that just 1 to 3 inches of the fenders remain above the surface. (On multi-axle trailers, this applies to the rearmost set of fenders.)

Try to avoid submerging the tow vehicle's rear-wheel hubs. While most vehicles will continue to run with their tailpipes submerged, this is a really bad idea and should be avoided. If the boat ramp gives you no choice but to submerge your vehicle's tailpipe (or the battery that powers the breakaway circuit on electric trailer brakes), don't. Pick another boat ramp or later look into fitting a hitch extender on your trailer (see Chapter 7 for more on hitch extenders).

When you've backed down as far as you need, make sure you stay there. Boating lore and websites are full of instances where trailer and tow vehicle have rolled all the way down the ramp together into the drink. A fully submerged tow vehicle will put a crimp in your plans for the day, and the next person waiting to use the ramp, while he or she may be amused with your situation, still won't be very happy about the consequences.

The best practice is to set the parking brake, put your automatic transmission in park (first gear if it's a standard shift), shut off the engine, and set chocks behind the rear wheels if they're on dry land (front wheels if not).

Don't back into the water too far. Note how this truck's wheel bearings and brakes are in the drink and the exhaust is submerged. If the engine stalls, the muffler will end up full of water.

Another approach is possible if you have a helper. One of you can launch the boat, while the other remains in the cab of the truck with the engine running and a heavy foot on the brake pedal. This will apply the brakes to all four wheels.

For most boats, once the stern is afloat, the boat can be pushed or powered rather easily off the trailer. Steeper ramps and roller-bunk trailers make this easier, while shallow-sloping ramps and carpeted bunks make it less so. (Indeed, boats on roller trailers could launch themselves with no other help than gravity, so make sure that you don't release the lock on the winch or safety chain before you're ready to launch at the water's edge.)

If you have a reversible electric winch and the boat will not roll rapidly off the back of the trailer, set the winch in reverse and pay out just enough slack to release tension on the cable or strap, so that you can unclip the hook from the bow eye. Then, controlling the boat with the dockline, you can push the boat back until it's fully afloat.

If, on the other hand, your trailer has rollers and the boat would launch itself

BOAT LAUNCH PARKING TIPS

Here are a few more items to take note of when parking your trailer and tow vehicle at a boat launch:

- Check the launch area's open hours. If the area is gate-controlled, you don't want to be locked in, ticketed, or towed if you return too late.
- Make sure your rig is parked entirely within a marked space and not obstructing the driving lanes, the ramp, or other parking spaces.
- Lock the trailer to the hitch ball.
- Leave no valuables in the tow vehicle. Bring them with you on the boat. Don't put your wallet in the glove box or your handbag under the seat. Thieves know where to look.
- Take any bags and place them out of sight, in the trunk, or beneath a cargo cover. Even if there's nothing of value in them, the sight of bags on the seats may prove intriguing to thieves, who may break in just to find out.
- Make sure the headlights are off.
- Lock the doors and take the keys.
- If you have a vehicle alarm, set it.

PRE-LAUNCH, LAUNCHING, AND RETRIEVAL CHECKLIST

PRE-LAUNCH PREPARATIONS

Conditions

— Examine the ramp for width, slope, surface, drop-off, and proximity of docks or beach
— Check the direction/speed of the wind and the current
— Examine the water for submerged debris

Trailer

— Remove and stow tie-down straps
— Remove bow safety chain/cable
— Disconnect electric harness (if applicable)

Boat

— Remove and stow engine brace or transom saver
— Install drain plug
— Check engine tilt mechanism
— Install removable running lights (if applicable)
— Test electrical system
— Test engine by starting for a couple seconds
— Load boat with gear: PFDs, emergency radio, charts, first-aid kit, ice chests, fishing gear, water toys, sunblock, sunglasses, extra clothes, music, food, and water
— Tie docklines to cleats and/or bow eye
— Hang fenders
— Run blowers (if applicable)

LAUNCHING

— Establish individual responsibilities for spotter, vehicle driver, and boat operator; clarify intended procedures
— Establish hand signals between spotter, vehicle driver, and boat operator
— Have all children and anyone unfamiliar with boats and docks don PFDs before walking on the dock
— Back trailer to water's edge, remove bow strap, and back trailer partway into water
— After boat operator starts engine and gives thumbs-up, continue backing trailer into water until boat stern floats free
— When boat is clear of trailer, pull forward up ramp and into designated parking area

RETRIEVAL

For retrieval, and prior to leaving the boat launch, most of these same items should be checked and, when necessary, reversed (e.g., install the engine brace, remove the drain plug, etc.).

forcefully if not restrained, don't rely on your own strength and a rope to keep it under control. A boat weighing 2,000 or more pounds, and moving backward at several feet per second, will easily yank you off your feet—in which case you'll be eating gravel as your boat gently drifts toward the middle of the lake. Instead, use the power of the winch to ease the boat all the way back into the water before releasing the hook.

If the ramp is adjacent to a dock, you can now walk with the end of the dock-line onto the dock and tie off. Likewise if you plan to temporarily beach the boat next to the ramp, you can simply walk it over and secure the line to something solid, such as a tree or an anchor embedded in the sand.

These options are not always available, however. At some unimproved boat launches, where there are no adjacent docks or beaches, you will have to launch at the ramp, then immediately move the boat to a remote location to board your passengers. Where this is the case, you will want the engine running as soon as the boat is afloat.

If you choose to power off the trailer, it pays to do some scouting first. Examine the slope of the ramp to ensure that the engine's prop and lower unit won't hit bottom when the boat comes off the trailer. Check that the water around the ramp is not excessively fouled with suspended sediment, weeds, or trash—you don't want to suck these into your engine's cooling circuit.

RETRIEVING THE BOAT

No matter how good or bad the day on the water was, first-time boaters rarely look forward to the boat loading process. Retrieving the boat is complicated by the fact that we're working against gravity, both in getting the boat onto the trailer, and getting the rig up the ramp. Additionally, you've probably had a long day, you're tired, and you might be tempted to skip a few steps or ignore a safety item or two. Here more than ever, it pays to have a good, fixed routine, so that you can do it all as efficiently and painlessly as possible.

As with launching, preparation is important. But unlike launching, most of the work will happen before you retrieve the boat from the water. Again, it's a matter of monopolizing the ramp for as short a time as possible while still performing the routine systematically and safely.

1. Get all the passengers out of the boat, except for the boat operator if you have one. If the dock area and ramp are not super busy and there are open spaces, dock the boat and off-load the passengers. Every passenger can take a handful of gear with them, rather than leaving it in the boat.
2. Get the boat trailer ready. Have the tie-down straps close at hand, and if you removed the winch handle, put it back on the winch.
3. Bring the tow vehicle down to the ramp. Have the boat operator power away from the dock and get in position to pull onto the trailer. At the same time, you get the trailer in line with the ramp and begin backing down. A spotter, while possibly helpful when backing, is not so important now as it was when you were launching the boat because your rear visibility is much better.

This trailer is too deep for easy retrieval. It's hard for the boat operator to see the bunks and difficult to get the boat centered on them.

4. Boats slide more easily on bunk carpets when the bunks are wet, so back in far enough to get them wet then pull forward until the top of the trailer fender is visible. If you back the trailer too deep into the water, the boat may not center itself on the bunks, because the hull will be floating above them rather than coming to rest on top of them. Better to be too shallow (you can always back in a bit more) than too deep. Most boats will center themselves fairly well if you can float them between a third and a half of their length onto the trailer before they are supported by the rollers or bunks.

5. Stop the tow vehicle and secure it on the slope. If you want to help guide the boat onto the trailer, get out of the vehicle and stand near the front and a bit off to one side of the trailer, so you are not in the direct path of the boat.

6. The boat may be either driven right onto the bunks or rollers under power, floated on, or winched on. A drive-on or float-on approach requires less physical effort (especially if you don't have an electric winch). However, these approaches are not allowed at some ramps because the prop wash can undercut the bottom of the lake at the end of the ramp, creating a deep drop-off.

Even where power-on and float-on approaches are possible, you may find it difficult to perfectly center the boat on the bunks or rollers, whereas winching allows for easier adjustments and more accurate positioning. You will have to experiment a bit to find out which approach

This is the proper depth for retrieval. The operator can see the front one-third of the bunks and drive the boat right onto them.

works best for your boat, how far you can float or drive onto the trailer before you have to winch it the rest of the way (if at all), and how far to submerge the trailer to make it happen.

7. If the water is shallow, the boat operator raises the engine or sterndrive enough to avoid hitting bottom, but not so far the propeller and water intake break of the surface.

8. The operator slowly approaches the trailer, taking both wind and current into consideration so that the hull lines up with the center of the trailer.

9. As the tow vehicle driver, you stand beside the trailer, using hand signals to help the operator center the boat. The boat operator uses just enough throttle to keep the boat's momentum pushing it up onto the trailer, but not so much as to slam into the bow stop. Use hand signals to let the boat operator know how far the bow eye is from the bow stop, since it's usually impossible to see the bow stop from the helm.

10. When the bow comes into contact with the bow stop, or within a couple of inches of it, signal the operator to kill the engine and trim it up.

11. Hook the winch strap into the bow eye and use the winch to pull the boat up tight against the bow stop.

12. If the operator cannot power the boat onto the trailer, or if you're doing a winch-up retrieval, it is your responsibility (the tow vehicle driver) to hook the winch strap to the boat's bow eye as soon as the boat operator brings the boat's bow within reach. If the slope of the ramp is slight and the operator can only get the bow over the bunks, you might have to pull out many feet of cable or strap from the winch, step onto the trailer, and walk all the way to the end of it to reach the bow eye. (Yes, this means you'll get wet.) Then operate the winch, bending down low enough to carefully observe how the boat slides up onto the bunks or rollers.

13. It's essential that your boat is centered on the trailer and properly supported by the bunks or rollers. Once the boat is most of the way up on the trailer, you won't easily be able to make side-to-side adjustments, unless the boat is *very* light. So if the boat begins to go off-center while you're winching, or it's being powered forward, stop, push it back toward the water, and straighten it out before bringing it in again.

14. Once the bow is firmly against the bow stop, fasten the bow tie-down or safety chain, but don't bother with transom or side straps at this time.

15. Drive the vehicle up the ramp, starting off with a light throttle so your tow vehicle doesn't lose traction. Better yet, if it's a four-wheel-drive vehicle, place it in 4WD mode.

As soon as you leave the immediate area of the ramp, find a place where you can perform the remainder of your retrieval and pre-tow tasks without interfering with other vehicles or boaters.

Pull the boat's drain plug and put it in its usual safe place. (Stand to the side when you pull it, or you may get a shoe full of water.) Ideally, the boat should be on a slight slope with the stern angled down to allow any water to drain before you get on the road.

LAUNCHING AND RETRIEVING PONTOON BOATS

Launching and retrieving procedures for pontoon boats are generally similar to those for regular monohull boats, with one significant difference. Pontoons weigh much less than other boats of similar dimensions, so they float higher in the water. The other side of this coin is that, because of their light weight, getting them on/off the trailer is far easier than a conventional boat of similar length.

Because pontoon boats float so high in the water, many pontoon trailers are designed to support them as low to the ground as possible. This float-on model supports the underside of the boat's deck, not the logs. (DAN ARMITAGE)

There are two ways to cope with these differences, based on the type of pontoon trailer you have. *Float-on trailers* are similar to conventional boat trailers, except in the configuration of the bunks. To get the lightweight boat to float on or off the bunks, you have to submerge the trailer quite far, so that the tops of the trailer fenders are just at, or even just below, the surface of the water. If the ramp has a shallow slope, this can be a problem.

Trailers with raising/lowering bunks are the best setup for launching and retrieving at a long, shallow ramps. Lower the pontoon from its raised towing position as the trailer enters the water. You should be able to power the bunks all the way down to their lowest position and float the pontoon boat free about the same time the tires slip below the water's surface.

Whether you have a float-on or raising/lowering trailer, I highly recommend it be equipped with side-loading guides. Pontoon boats don't have V-shaped hulls that self-align, to a degree, with bunks that have been properly set up for a V-hull. Loading a pontoon boat is more akin to floating or pulling a log raft onto a flat trailer, except the bunks are relatively narrow, and the pontoons must be placed on them precisely to be properly supported. The side guides make the loading process easier as they help center the pontoon boat on the trailer as you winch or pull it to the winch stand/bow stop. They are especially handy on windy afternoons or when retrieving your 'toon from a river.

After retrieving your pontoon boat, and using the appropriate tie-down straps, secure the bow-eye strap to the winch stand and each corner of the pontoon boat to the trailer. On larger pontoon boats, place at least one ratchet-style strap over each outer log, securing it to the trailer.

Make all the usual preparations before driving off, just as you did when you left home that day. These include fastening the transom and side straps, connecting the trailer lights, checking the lights and brakes, and securing everything inside the boat to keep it from sliding around or flying out. Refer to Chapter 5 for a complete checklist and description of procedures. I also like to take this time to wipe down the boat to prevent water spots.

Retrieving Solo

Here's how to retrieve a boat solo where there is a dock immediately adjacent to the ramp:

1. Bring the boat to the dock and tie up. Tie the bow line to the bow eye.
2. Get the tow vehicle and back the trailer into the water so that least two thirds of the bunks are under water and the trailer is parallel to the dock and within 1 to 2 feet from it.
3. Park and secure the tow vehicle on the ramp.
4. Go back to the boat, take the bow line in hand, and untie the dockline.
5. Standing on the dock, hold on to the coil of bow line, and gently push the boat out away from the dock.
6. Quickly walk up the dock to the front of the trailer, guiding the boat toward the trailer.
7. Once you're in position at the tongue of the trailer, continue to pull the boat toward you, guiding it onto the bunks.
8. When the boat is centered and pulled up as far as you can manage, run the winch strap out to the bow eye and use the winch to finish the loading job.

Power loading solo requires more finesse, but less muscle, than manual loading. It may be difficult to see the trailer from the helm of the boat, although side guides on the trailer can ease this problem somewhat. Additionally, you won't know if the boat is centered on the rollers or bunks until you've driven onto the trailer and stepped out of the cockpit. Nonetheless, with practice, many people learn to do this almost as second nature.

To power load the boat solo:

1. Back the trailer down the ramp and into the water. Don't have the trailer so deep that you could drive the boat all the way to the bow stop, because you simply can't see the bow stop from the helm.
2. Drive the boat onto the middle of the trailer until it comes firmly up on the bunks or rollers.
3. Once the boat is within a foot or two of the bow stop—and if the bow of the boat is low enough—step from the cockpit onto the bow, lean over, and hook the winch to the bow eye.
4. If you can't reach the winch strap from the bow, step down to the trailer

RETRIEVAL TIPS FOR SAILBOATS

Before floating or winching a sailboat onto its trailer, raise the centerboard or lifting keel all the way. Then after you've secured the boat on the trailer, lower the keel so it rests on a cross member of the trailer.

You may find it convenient to remove the rudder while the boat is still afloat, or you can wait until it's on the trailer. If you retrieve with the rudder on, make sure it's in the kicked-up position.

to complete the job. The goal is to do the whole thing without getting your feet soaked.

I have seen avid boaters launch and retrieve boats solo faster than many boaters do with the help of a couple people. Regardless of method, familiarity with your boat, practice, and timing will determine how easy self-loading becomes for you. Once you're proficient, you can go boating anytime you want, whether or not friends or family are available.

LAUNCHING AND RETRIEVING IN WIND OR CURRENT

A crosswind or river current can make launching and retrieving more difficult, and if both are present and moving in the same direction, then their force, of course, is additive. It's impossible to give simple rules about whether the wind or the current will affect the boat more if they are going in different directions. This is something that you, as the boatowner, can only learn from experiencing

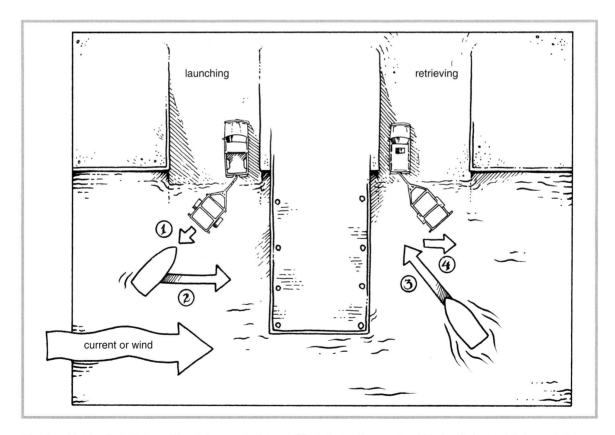

When launching, face the trailer toward the wind or current. (1) Come off the trailer into the current, and (2) allow the boat to drift down onto the dock. When retrieving, face the trailer away from the wind or current. Point the boat upstream of the trailer (3), and allow the current to push it downstream (4) so that the bow meets the trailer at the proper time. (CHRISTOPHER HOYT)

different conditions. In the discussion that follows, when I refer to the force or direction of the wind/current, I mean whichever one has the dominant effect on your boat at that time.

When launching with a crosswind/current, choose a lane or position the trailer so that the wind/current will push the boat toward the dock. If you are launching with the engine, make sure it's warmed up before the boat comes free from the trailer. If the engine stalls, the boat may drift into the dock harder than you'd like.

Wherever possible, position the trailer so that the boat will launch with the wind/current—in other words, you should be pushing the transom with the flow. Especially with current, the moment your stern floats free, it will start to swing downwind/downcurrent. As the boat floats off the trailer the boat operator can power into the current, getting quick control.

The tricky part of this is to position the trailer askew on the ramp, possibly at a fairly sharp angle, without interfering with other users of the ramp. Although this is really just another backing-and-turning maneuver, it requires more driving finesse than usual, because you're working within a fairly narrow space on a downhill slope. You'll only gain confidence by practicing, so give it a try some day when it's quiet at the boat ramp, even if the wind or current doesn't make it necessary.

When retrieving the boat, the strategy is the same. You'll be able to control your boat much better when working into the wind/current than with it, so angle the trailer so that the taillights face downwind/downcurrent. The boat operator should point the boat somewhat upstream of the back of the trailer. Then as she or he moves the boat forward, the wind/current will push it a bit downstream so the bow meets the trailer at just the right time.

LAUNCH RAMP ETIQUETTE

People are constantly finding new ways to do things wrong when launching and retrieving boats, and the antics that occur at any busy boat ramp on a warm summer weekend are worthy of *America's Funniest Home Videos*.

But what is humorous to the casual observer can be infuriating to the serious boater who's waiting in line for a chance at the ramp. Simply put, taking too long at the ramp is impolite. The best way to be a responsible boat-ramp user is to practice the skills until you can launch and retrieve efficiently and effectively.

Here are some more points of etiquette that will make you a welcome member of the boat-ramp fraternity:

- When using a ramp at night, turn off your headlights. They can be blinding to anyone trying to back onto the ramp beside you. Leave your parking lights on so they can see you.
- Prepare the boat and trailer for the launch or retrieval before you pull onto the ramp. Undo the straps, load the gear, remove the transom saver, put in the drain plug, etc. Go through the entire checklist in the parking lot so you're not running around looking for things, wasting time and motion on the ramp.
- Learn to back straight and centered onto the ramp so that you're not crowding an adjacent lane.

- Learn the parameters of your truck and trailer, so you know how far to back down without having to get in and out of the truck a half-dozen times.
- Use a spotter when backing down the ramp to launch. It's safer for everyone around you.
- If something does go wrong on the ramp that will take a while to sort out, if possible, pull out and give the next guy a chance.
- Drive slowly around boat launches. There are lots of kids running around as well as a lot of distracted people.
- Park your rig neatly in a designated spot, making sure not to block the driving lanes.
- Offer help to those who need it.
- Be willing to accept help when you need it, or when it would make the process go faster.

WHEN YOU GET HOME

After a long day of boating and driving, it can be dismaying to be faced with another set of tasks. Do them anyway—your boat will be the better for it, and you'll feel a lot better when you're done.

- Park the trailer where it is out of plain sight if possible. This is an extremely simple theft deterrent. If a potential thief can't see the target, there's no target. Of course, using a padlock in the hitch-lockpin hole or locking the trailer to a solid object will be more effective.
- Unhitching the trailer is the reverse of hitching it. Back it into place, lower the tongue jack, chock the wheels, and disconnect all of the various connections.
- Raise the tongue so the boat is tilted slightly astern. Leave the drain plug out, so any water that enters the hull will drain.
- Remove all perishable and stealable gear and supplies.
- Rinse off the boat and trailer, and flush the brakes.
- Dry the wiring harness connector, place a bit of petroleum jelly on the contacts, and place a plastic bag over the plug.
- Install a boat cover if you have one.
- Put a hitch lock or padlock on the trailer coupler latch.

Trailering Sailboats

S everal special considerations apply to trailering, launching, and retrieving sailboats. Sailboats have rigs that must be broken down for travel and set up for sailing. Many have transom-mounted rudders that should be removed for trailering and mounted for use. Deep keels make launching and retrieving problematic. And the additional height of a deep fixed keel imposes special requirements on trailer hardware and driving.

All that said, there are certainly more similarities than differences between sailboat and powerboat trailering. Most of the procedures are identical—to the extent that sailboat owners should read all the preceding chapters for the scoop on standard hardware and procedures. With a few important exceptions, driving, launching, and retrieving procedures are the same, and tow vehicle and hitch considerations are identical for the two types of boats.

SAILBOAT TRAILERS

Manufacturers often design sailboat trailers to be substantially different from powerboat trailers, and these differences require some adaptations in driving, launching, and retrieving. This is more the case with trailers for keelboats, and less so for lightweight sailboats, which have no large, fixed bottom appendages.

Fixed-keel boats are inevitably taller than powerboats or sailboats with centerboards or lifting keels, and in spite of the weight of the ballast down low, keelboats are subject to tipping over while most powerboats are not. Trailers for keelboats, therefore, must have supports that reach up on both sides of the keel to the bottom of the hull. Some trailers use raised bunks, while others use screw pads or poppets. If raised bunks are used, they are carefully curved to fit the shape of the hull, rather than the simple, straight bunks found on powerboat trailers. In some cases, the sailboat trailer's bunks have *breaks* that allow the boat to be lifted in slings by a crane.

If screw pads are used, the boat's positioning on the trailer is likely to be even more critical than usual, since they support the boat in only four or six discrete locations. These locations must be carefully identified as strong points on the hull—for example, areas that are reinforced on the boat's interior by bulkheads. If the screw pads bear on unsupported areas of the hull, the laminates or planks could be damaged by either long-term, repeated flexing or a single

On sailboat trailers, the raised bunks are usually curved to fit the shape of the hull. (PETER DUPRE/AUTOWORD)

catastrophic impact, as might occur if the trailer were to hit a curb or a large pothole.

Bunks or screw pads, however, do not support most of the weight of a keelboat. Their purpose is to keep the boat upright, while the majority of the weight is borne on the trailer frame directly beneath the keel. Obviously, this part of the trailer must be engineered to bear this heavy concentration of weight.

In contrast, trailers for shallow-draft boats with lifting keels, swing keels, or centerboards support the boat in a manner similar to powerboat trailers, using conventional bunks or rollers. Even they, however, should have a cross member to support the weight of the liftable ballast, which should be lowered before driving.

This last point is important. Otherwise, the weight of the swing keel will rest entirely on a single pivot bolt and the keel's lifting mechanism, which, in many cases, relies on a single, relatively lightweight cable. Driving the boat over the road with the keel's weight supported by its pivot bolt and lifting mechanism can easily result in expensive damage to both, as well as to the fiberglass trunk through which the pivot bolt passes.

Even if the boat has a relatively lightweight centerboard, it is still worthwhile to lower the board before driving, if only to protect the lifting pendant. Having a special support on the trailer, however, is less critical. If your trailer lacks a support as an integral part of the frame, you may be able to bolt a piece of 2×4 or 2×6 lumber across the frame to act as a support. Don't drill the trailer frame to make the attachment. Use U-bolts or pairs of long bolts on both sides of each of the trailer's rails to clamp the timber to the frame from above and below.

Regardless of whether your boat has a lightweight centerboard or a heavy lifting or swing keel, remember to raise it before attempting to launch or retrieve the boat, and make lowering it part of your checklist before driving away. The board should remain in the down position on the trailer's cross member between trips and during long periods of storage.

Buying a Sailboat Trailer

When a new sailboat is sold with a trailer, you can be confident that the boat manufacturer

Achieving the correct positioning for the screw pads is critical to properly supporting a deep-keel hull. Note the extra-tall bow stop. (PETER DUPRE/AUTOWORD)

has thought carefully about (1) the precise placement of supports to keep the boat safely in position, and (2) the fore-and-aft balance of the boat on the trailer in relation to the trailer's tongue weight (TW). (As covered in Chapter 3, the norm for TW is 5 to 10 percent of its gross total weight or GTW.) Not so if you purchase a trailer separately, as may be the case if you buy a used boat or build one for yourself, or have to replace an old, decrepit trailer that's beyond restoration.

Sailboat trailers tend to be more specialized and less generic than powerboat trailers, and it's not possible to accurately recommend a trailer type based simply on the boat's length and weight. You'll need to find a trailer manufacturer that either offers models for your boat or builds custom trailers.

The weight of a ballasted keel rests on the trailer frame. Note the keel guides that help position the boat.
(PETER DUPRE/AUTOWORD)

The best approach to buying a trailer for an existing sailboat is to contact the sailboat manufacturer, or the trailer manufacturer used by the sailboat builder, and order one for your specific model of boat. Even if your boat is no longer in production, the trailer manufacturer probably has all the specifications in hand and can build one precisely fitted to it. Make sure you specify the exact model and year of your hull, because production boat manufacturers often make minor changes in hull shape or construction details from year to year.

Even if the original trailer manufacturer is out of business, others may offer properly fitted trailers if your sailboat is a popular model. It may take some research and a lot of e-mails or phone calls to find out.

However, if your sailboat is not a garden-variety model, you'll need to order a custom-built unit, and to do that you must measure your boat out of the water. The builder will need to know the make and model of the vessel and its measurements, but neither of you should rely on measurements printed in the manufacturer's sales literature, owner's manual, or blueprints. Sailboat builders are famous for changing hull specs during production runs, and printed measurements may not be accurate for your specific hull.

Measuring your sailboat for a trailer is akin to a tailor fitting you for a custom suit. A lot of measurements are needed to get a good fit. Among the measurements the trailer builder will need are the following:

- Length on deck (LOD) measured from the tip of the bow to the center of the stern
- Length overall (LOA)
- Maximum beam
- Distance from the front of the keel to the stern
- Distance from the back of the keel to the stern
- Distance from the bottom of the keel to the chine or to a point 30 inches outboard of the keel

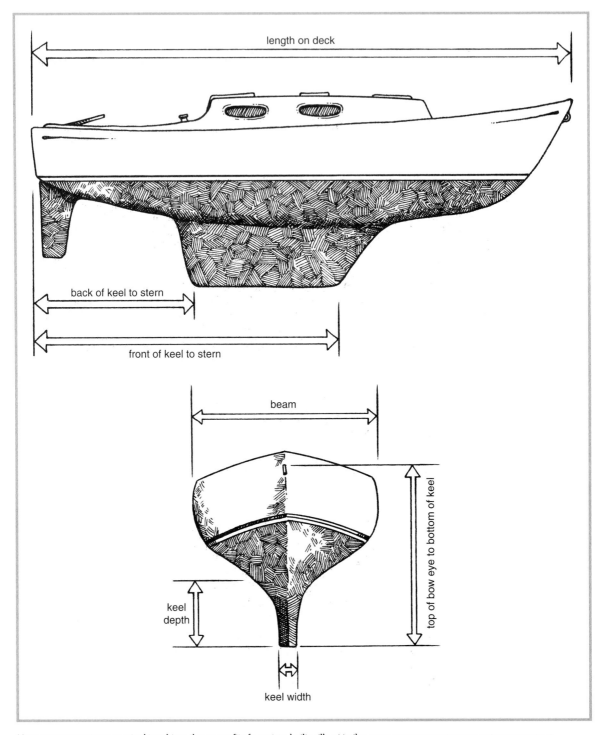

Many measurements are required to achieve the proper fit of a custom-built sailboat trailer. (PETER DUPRE/AUTOWORD, DRAWN BY CHRISTOPHER HOYT)

- Distance from the bottom of the keel to the top of the bow eye
- Keel depth
- Keel width at its widest point
- Distance between twin keels, if applicable
- Weight of the boat with full tanks (including ballast), engine, and gear

Depending upon your boat model and the trailer builder, you may need more measurements than those listed above. Sending along photos of your boat may be helpful. The manufacturer will also want to know about your tow vehicle's tow ratings and your hitch class.

You'll need to make some decisions with the manufacturer on trailer options:

- Material of construction: painted or galvanized steel or aluminum
- Number of axles
- Type of brakes: surge, electric, or electric/hydraulic
- Extra-tall winch stand
- Winch type and capacity: manual or electric, one- or two-speed
- Adjustable-height bow stop
- Raised bunks (with or without cutouts for lifting slings) or screw pads
- Keel and side guides
- Ladder
- Spare tire bracket
- Toolbox
- Auxiliary lighting
- Diamond-plate step
- Mast-raising apparatus

You also might want to specify brackets to carry the mast and boom, in which case you'll need to know the length, width, and front-to-back dimensions of the spars.

If your boat has a deep keel, you should also consider adding a trailer tongue extension, such as those made by Extend A Hitch (see Appendix A for contact information). These allow you to back the trailer into deeper water for launch without having to put the tow vehicle door-deep in the water.

Trailer manufacturers vary from large and well-established companies that are part of major public corporations to mom-and-pop welding and fabrication shops that build trailers as a sideline. Regardless of their size, it is wise to stick with reputable companies, with experience in sailboat trailers in particular. Any trailer you buy must meet Department of Transportation (DOT) specifications and should have a DOT sticker affixed to the frame. NMMA-certified trailers usually carry an NMMA sticker as well.

A ladder can be a useful, or even essential, accessory on a trailer for a keelboat. (PETER DUPRE/AUTOWORD)

A long hitch extension makes it possible to launch a deep-keel sailboat without backing the truck into the water. (PETER DUPRE/AUTOWORD)

Positioning the Boat on the Trailer

Unless your sailboat is a lightweight, shallow boat like a Sunfish, Laser, or Hobie Cat, you'll probably need a boatyard with a travel lift or hoist to place your sailboat on your new trailer. Care must be taken to ensure that the vessel is properly positioned and supported. Even with all the information you provided and the most precise fabrication, you may still need to make some adjustments:

- Confirm the boat is supported securely. If the boat has a heavy ballast keel, make sure that the keel is resting solidly on the trailer. The side supports should be firm against the bottom to prevent any possible side-to-side movement, but they should not bear significant weight. You don't want the ballast keel hanging from the hull. If you see any deflection of the hull's sides or bottom, the side supports are too high and must be adjusted.
- Adjust the winch stand so the bow eye is positioned below the bow chock or stop. The winch line should feed directly to the bow eye without interference, pulling forward and down so you can crank the bow snugly into the bow chock.
- Confirm that the trailer's TW is 7 to 10 percent of its GTW. Adjustments can be made by moving the boat forward or aft on the trailer, or by redistributing weight in the boat.

Obviously, moving gear inside the boat is the easier approach, and moving heavy weights into or out of the extreme ends of the boat can have a dramatic effect. If the TW is too light, and you keep an outboard on the stern, try moving it amidships. (Storing the outboard inside the boat also prevents stress to the bracket and acts as a theft deterrent.) If TW is excessive, try moving heavy ground tackle out of the chain locker in the forepeak. Other easily movable weights may include gas cans and large ice chests. The position of your freshwater and holding tanks, and whether they are full or empty, may also make a big difference.

If moving gear around does not suffice, you may need to reposition the boat on the trailer. Make sure you move the winch stand accordingly so that the bow remains snug in the chock. Shallow-draft boats that sit on bunks can often be simply slid forward or back. If the boat has a deep keel and the trailer uses screw pads, move the pads while ensuring they continue to bear against the same areas of the hull. If you need to reposition the boat by more than a few inches to achieve the proper TW, something is wrong, and you should contact the trailer builder for advice. It may be that the tongue is the wrong length or the axles were mounted incorrectly.

While powerboats sit *on* the trailer, deep-keel sailboats seem to sit *in* them, because of the higher side supports. Don't allow this to lull you into thinking that the boat is secure just sitting there. All boats need to be strapped securely to the trailer, with webbing straps running from both sides of the hull to the trailer.

LAUNCHING AND RETRIEVING

With the exception of rigging concerns, launching a sailboat without a deep fixed keel is identical to launching a powerboat of comparable weight, as we covered in Chapter 6. (Note the advisability of rigging the boat while it is still on the trailer, and be especially cautious of overhead obstructions such as tree limbs, signs, and electrical wires.) However, special considerations apply to launching and retrieving deep-keel boats.

Launching a Deep-Keel Sailboat

It is often impossible to power a deep-keel sailboat off its trailer. Additionally, its high topsides generally prevent you from standing on the trailer, pushing the boat off, and clambering aboard as it drifts aft. Then once the boat is afloat, facing the shore and only a few feet away from it, it's virtually impossible to sail the boat to the dock, so if your boat doesn't have an engine, someone who's not on board will have to lead the boat by means of a dockline tied to a bow cleat.

That pretty much describes the procedure, which isn't complicated. If you're working with a helper, attach a long dockline to a bow cleat and place fenders along one side of the hull before you ease the boat down with the winch. When the boat's afloat, the person who's holding the dockline unhooks the winch from the bow eye and leads the boat to the dock, while the other reels in the winch cable and then pulls the trailer off the ramp.

If you're working alone, you'll have to trot back to the truck and take care of things as soon as the boat is secure at the dock. If the boat has an engine, make sure that all docklines are out of the water before backing away from the trailer under power.

Retrieving a Deep-Keel Sailboat

While you may be able to launch solo, you'll find a helper is a necessity during retrieval, for several reasons. The far-aft helm position and the overhanging bow on most sailboats obstructs your view of the trailer once you get close. Having someone on land giving hand signals to the helm is neither very accurate nor effective. Furthermore, deep-keel sailboats usually cannot be floated or driven onto their trailers as high as powerboats. It is usually necessary, therefore, to winch the boat forward onto the trailer. But again, given the geometry of a deep-keel sailboat, it's almost impossible to do this single-handed: you just can't step

Sometimes, you just have to get wet to get the boat lined up on the trailer. Those times are a lot more frequent with deep-keel sailboats.

off the deck of a sailboat onto any part of the trailer that's not a couple of feet under water. It is much better, therefore, to have a helper on land to lead the boat onto the trailer with a dockline from the bow.

Retrieval with a helper is as follows:

1. The helper prepares by unreeling enough winch strap to reach the end of the trailer.
2. If the boat is being powered up to the trailer, someone on board throws the bow line to the helper. Otherwise, the helper leads the boat by the dockline all the way from the dock to the trailer.
3. If the dock is crowded, or the sailboat is drifting with a side wind, it may be necessary for the helper to go in the water to help line up the boat. (Just pray the water isn't ice cold or neck deep, either of which can ruin an otherwise great outing.)
4. In either case, once the boat is positioned at the end of the trailer, the helper pulls the boat up with the dockline, guiding the keel onto the trailer's keel support.
5. When the boat is as far forward as it can go by hand, the helper attaches the winch strap to the bow eye and winches the boat up to the chock.
6. If winching is difficult, don't try to overcome the resistance by brute force— there is an excellent chance of damaging something. Instead, the helper stops and examines the situation, and if necessary, pushes the boat back into the water somewhat and realigns it before trying again.
7. Once the boat is safely in position, but before you drive the truck up the ramp, gather up the bow dockline from the water and secure it so that it can't get caught under the trailer wheels.

Hitch Extenders

As mentioned briefly above, a hitch extender is a supplemental tongue and coupler that mounts beneath the trailer frame. It can be extremely useful on a trailer for a keel sailboat. When extended, it typically adds between 5 and 10 feet to the front end of the trailer, allowing the trailer to be backed that much farther into the water before submerging the tow vehicle's wheel hubs. Do not use hitch extenders for towing on the highway—they are for boat-ramp use only.

Using a hitch extender during launch and retrieval is straightforward:

1. Just before you back onto the ramp, park the tow vehicle, put down the tongue jack, and unhitch the trailer.
2. Pull the tow vehicle forward to accommodate the length of the extender.
3. Pull the locking pin on the extender, and pull the extender out to its full length.

4. Reinsert the locking pin in the extended position and raise the tongue jack until the hitch ball fits under the extender's ball coupler.
5. Hitch the trailer and launch the boat.
6. After retrieving the boat, reverse the procedure to retract the extender.

If your rig is too long for the parking spaces at the boat launch with the extender deployed, have the courtesy to retract it when parking, then redeploy it for retrieval.

Tilt-Bed Trailers

Tilt-bed trailers have a hinge in the middle that allows you to lower the back half of the trailer and get the boat deeper into the water without having to back the trailer farther in. These have passed out of fashion on boat trailers, because they never truly delivered the ease of launching and retrieving manufacturers promised. However, there are still a few around, and you might buy a used boat complete with an old one. (Tilt-beds remain popular on other types of trailers, including those built for snowmobiles, motorcycles, and general hauling.)
To use a tilt-bed trailer:

1. Back your vehicle down the ramp as far as practical in the usual manner.
2. Tie a long dockline to a bow cleat.
3. Release the tilt bed. Locking mechanisms vary, but they usually consist of pulling a pin and releasing a latch. With the latch released, the back of the trailer will tilt down, and the boat will be held in place by the winch strap.
4. Release the winch lock and use the winch to control the boat as it slips back into the water.
5. When the bow reaches the back end of the trailer, unhook the winch strap from the bow eye and use the dockline to control the boat.
6. Raise the tilt bed before driving off the ramp.

Retrieval is just as simple:

1. Back onto the ramp and release the tilt bed.
2. Run the winch strap out to the end of the trailer, but don't attach it to the boat yet.
3. Pull the boat as far as possible onto the trailer with the dockline, then hook the winch strap to the bow eye and pull the boat up.
4. The trailer bed will automatically tilt back up.
5. Secure the locking mechanism before driving off the ramp.

If you own a tilt-bed trailer, make checking the locking mechanism an essential part of your pre-towing checklist.

RIGGING ISSUES

Rigs differ too greatly for me to give detailed instructions on how to set them up. If in doubt how to rig your boat, contact the manufacturer or join an Internet discussion group devoted to your boat model. I can, however, provide some rigging-related guidance as it relates to towing.

You will require some means of transporting the mast and boom. Some trailers have special cradles or brackets for this purpose. If your trailer doesn't, you can easily fabricate brackets from strap steel, lumber, or plywood and bolt them to the trailer frame. Be sure to pad the brackets with scraps of carpet to protect the spar's anodized finish or varnish, and to securely lash the spars in their brackets prior to travel.

If your trailer lacks room to carry the spars beside or beneath the boat, you'll need to carry them on deck. Although you can lash spars to the roof of the cabin house and the bow and stern pulpits, this is a poor solution, as it requires time and effort (and excellent knot-tying skills) to do the job properly. And if not done well, the spars may come partially or entirely loose in transit, with results that are not difficult to imagine.

A better approach, therefore, is to fabricate a mast crutch or two. This is a temporary bracket designed to hold the spars secure. It can be as simple as a straight, vertical board, shaped to accept the mast at the top, and tapered to fit into flat stainless steel brackets fastened to the back of the cockpit or the transom. Some sailboat owners bolt a set of pintles to the crutch and use the gudgeons on the transom to hold them. Another option is a pair of boards with a bolt that allows them to move like scissors. The (padded) lower ends rest against the sides of the cockpit, and the crutch takes the shape of an X, with its lower legs wider and taller than its upper ones. The mast rests in the V between the upper legs.

You can use a similar method to support the forward end of the mast at or near the bow pulpit and, if necessary, make a simple cradle to rest securely on the cabin house room. The mast step also makes an excellent mounting point for a support.

With proper crutches and cradles in place, it is a much simpler affair to tie the spars down securely. The mast should travel on the boat or the trailer with its bottom end facing toward the bow. Take care to avoid kinking the shrouds and stays at all times during setup, breakdown, and preparation for travel. Even a small kink in a wire stay will weaken it considerably. For travel, secure the wires with bungee cords or hook-and-loop fabric straps (e.g., Velcro) at intervals along the length of the mast. Wind the lower ends together in large-diameter loops and secure them so they do not flail in the wind or slap against anything.

As I've already mentioned, watch out for obstructions before stepping the mast. You must have a clear, safe path between your rigged boat sitting on its trailer and the boat ramp. Having the deck sloping slightly downhill toward the bow makes securing the mast easier, as you shall see below:

1. Slide the mast aft until its bottom is over the mast step.
2. Make sure the forward face of the mast is up, then bolt the base of the mast to the step. Do not overtighten the bolt, or you'll deform the mast extrusion or make the hinge too tight.
3. Check that the shrouds and stays are properly secured to the mast fittings, and the halyards are in place, with both ends of the halyards secured near the base of the mast.

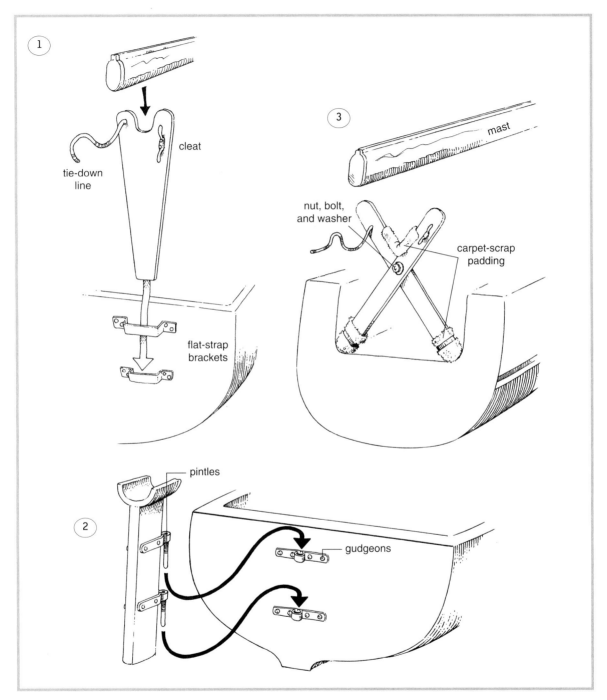

Three good homemade mast crutches: (1) flat, stainless steel, strap brackets on the transom, (2) pintles on the crutch fit into the rudder gudgeons on the transom, and (3) a scissors-style arrangement that fits between the cockpit seats. (CHRISTOPHER HOYT)

4. Attach the shrouds to the chain plates and tilt the mast up and forward on its hinge bolt. This, of course, is the hard part. Depending upon the size of your mast and your own strength and agility, you may need one or more helpers, mechanical assistance, or both.

5. As the mast goes up, keep a close watch on the shrouds to make sure they don't become kinked or get caught on any obstructions.

6. When the mast is upright, apply constant forward pressure against it. This will allow the shrouds to keep it from falling to the sides and forward. If the boat is tilted slightly down toward the bow, gravity will help. If not, someone must apply pressure manually to attach the forestay.

   If you are working by yourself, an easy way to do this is to take either the lower end of the topping lift, or both ends of one of the halyards, bring them forward, and tie them off firmly with some tension to the bow pulpit or something similar. This will keep forward pressure on the mast while you fasten the bottom end of the forestay to the fitting on the deck.

7. Double-check the bottoms of the shrouds and stays to make sure that clevis pins are in place and locked with cotters or split rings.

8. Attach the boom and bend on the sails. Don't raise the sails—use bungee cords to keep them bundled up. You don't want them blowing around during the launch.

Unrigging the boat and preparing the rig for travel follows much the same procedures but in reverse order. Be even more careful when lowering the mast than you were when raising it. It is easy to allow the weight to get away from you.

8

Maintenance

As a boatowner, you already know that maintenance is a fact of life. Skimp on maintenance, and your former pride and joy will rapidly begin to look shabby, run poorly, and lose resale value. The same holds true for your entire towing rig: the tow vehicle, hitch, and trailer. Even brand-new towing packages of the highest quality require regular maintenance to stay reliable and safe.

Much of what comes under the heading of *maintenance* is really inspection, to determine whether or not you need to do additional work. For example, you should regularly check the tires on your tow vehicle or trailer for even tread wear, sidewall cracks, and proper inflation. Usually, all will be well. At times, however, you will need to add air to maintain tire pressure; rotate the tires on your tow vehicle and trailer; and even replace tires when they become too old, worn, or damaged.

The same goes for many other components and systems throughout the tow rig. It's essential to inspect them regularly. By doing so, you will often catch small problems before they become big, expensive ones.

THE TOW VEHICLE

I won't go into all the details of what you need to do to keep a tow vehicle running under normal (i.e., nontowing) conditions. As a motor vehicle owner, you probably already know and follow the basics of vehicle maintenance as outlined in your owner's manual. If you don't, get out that manual and read it.

Few owner's manuals, however, pay much attention to the special needs of vehicles that are used for towing. Of particular importance are the issues of engine and transmission cooling and tires.

Engine Cooling

Every automaker goes to great lengths to ensure their engines and transmissions are adequately cooled for use in fairly extreme conditions. They take their vehicles to the desert Southwest in midsummer, load them to the maximum gross vehicle weight rating (GVWR), and drive them up the steepest grades in triple-digit heat, time and time again. Such testing is done to make sure the cooling systems are capable of sustaining operating temperatures below the danger zones for both engine oils and transmission fluids in extreme conditions.

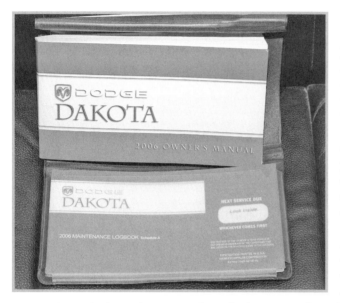

Your owner's manual is the best source of information on basic maintenance requirements and intervals.

Engines are cooled in two ways. One is through the engine coolant, which is pumped through intricately cast passages in the engine block and cylinder head(s) and out to the radiator. There the heat is dissipated via the airflow over the radiator tubes.

The other cooling system is the engine oil, which constantly circulates from the oil pan or sump, over and around all the engine's internal moving parts, through the oil filter, and back to the sump, which is exposed to the air.

But even with these two systems, standard cooling systems are often insufficient to ensure the longevity of the engine and transmission in a tow vehicle. The reason is towing imposes its own set of extreme conditions on the vehicle. Naturally, when towing a load, the engine works harder, which means that it burns more fuel. This, in turn, generates more heat, which, if not properly dissipated, can drastically reduce the lubricating effectiveness of the engine oil. This loss of lubrication generates *even more* heat, leading to the accelerated wear of a number of the engine's internal components.

Most engine and oil manufacturers recommend maximum oil temperatures between 180°F and 200°F. A rule of thumb states that for every 10°C (approx. 18°F) increase in temperature above its recommended operating temperature, the length of time a motor oil can do its job optimally is cut in half. So if the engine and oil manufacturers recommend 180°F, but the actual operating temperature is 198°F, the oil will have to be changed twice as often to provide adequate lubrication. If the oil temperature goes up to 216°F, its life is cut in half again.

Even though automakers commonly specify oil-change intervals of 6,000 to 10,000 miles, many owners stick to the old, conservative 3,000-mile schedule. Given the quality of today's engines and oil formulations, virtually all automotive experts agree that this is unnecessary and wasteful, under normal circumstances.

But if your engine is burdened with a towing a trailer, your vehicle falls under what is usually referred to as Maintenance Schedule "B" in the owner's manual, indicating "severe use." Thus, it is not just prudent to change your tow vehicle's engine oil every 3,000 miles—maintaining your warranty may require that you do so.

Recognizing the need for better engine cooling in tow vehicles, automakers offer various cooling upgrades within their optional towing packages. The cooling component of a towing package may include some or all of the following:

- larger or higher-efficiency radiator
- special radiator shroud for improved airflow
- auxiliary oil cooler
- transmission cooler

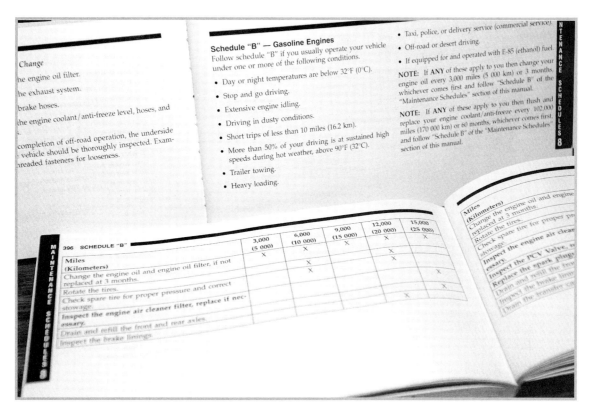

Follow the automaker's recommendations for severe use to determine the best intervals for oil changes and other maintenance tasks on your tow vehicle.

When buying a new tow vehicle, you should certainly purchase the optional towing package. But even this may not be sufficient, since not all towing packages include all of these features. Although a new factory cooling package should keep the operating temperatures below the point where the engine oil or transmission fluid will rapidly lose their ability to cool and provide lubrication, it may still allow temperatures to rise well above normal driving temperatures.

This situation is what I call the *slow death zone*, in which the drivetrain will live long enough to survive the warranty period, but not as long as it really should. This could mean the difference between needing main bearings, a ring job, or a transmission rebuild at 60,000 miles versus 120,000 miles or more.

Whether buying a new or used vehicle, therefore, check the towing package and see what it includes. If an oil cooler isn't included, add one to keep your truck out of the slow death zone. Aftermarket units are available for generic applications as well as specific vehicles and often sell for $100 to $300. This is cheap insurance to keep your vehicle running longer. Some will reduce oil temperatures by as much as 30°F under certain conditions.

Installing an auxiliary oil cooler is a viable job for most automotive do-it-yourselfers.

Installation tends to be fairly simple and is a suitable job for most do-it-yourselfers:

1. Remove the engine's oil filter.
2. Screw the special fitting into the place for the oil filter.
3. Reinstall the oil filter on top of the fitting. Two high-temperature hoses run from the fitting to the cooler, which is like a small radiator.
4. Mount the cooler anywhere inside the engine compartment where it will receive a good flow of cooling air when the vehicle is moving. Often, the easiest place to the mount the cooler is on the front of the radiator. While this location is not ideal with regard to heat transfer, it does afford the best airflow and works sufficiently well in most installations.

Some oil coolers have built-in electric fans, which somewhat reduce the need for natural airflow. Of course, you have to connect these to the vehicle's electrical system, but this is a simple two-wire job that makes it easy for anyone to install.

Transmission Cooling

Similar issues apply to automatic transmissions, which generate heat due to friction between gears and clutch packs. The heavier the load, the more friction and heat that are generated. Therefore, proper cooling is an important issue for transmissions, and inadequate cooling is the cause of 90 percent of all automatic transmission failures.

Transmissions depend upon transmission fluid for internal cooling, which normally runs considerably cooler than engine oil. External cooling, however, is only provided by the transmission's heavily ribbed case. For tow vehicles, therefore, an external cooler is an important addition.

Transmission Cooler

Much like the supplemental engine oil coolers, transmission coolers are often included, and these tend to work well. As with oil coolers, you should add one to your vehicle if it's not already equipped with one. Manufacturers such as B&M, Perma-Cool, Hayden, TCI, and others claim that a drop of 20 degrees in fluid temperature can double the life of the transmission. (See Appendix A for oil cooler and transmission cooler suppliers.)

Although the radiator is a common mounting location, it may get too crowded with two supplemental coolers on front. Also three heat-dissipating units in close proximity will not operate with optimum effectiveness.

TCI claims that by mounting the transmission cooler in front of the air-conditioning condenser, the cooler will function to 100 percent efficiency. This drops to 75 percent when

Replacing an old transmission cooler with a new, larger one.

the cooler is mounted between the air-conditioning condenser and the radiator, and 60 percent when mounted between the radiator and the fan. If there's no good place to mount the transmission cooler inside the engine compartment, look for a safe mounting location behind the bumper, front air dam, or some other location exposed to a flow of fresh air but protected from stone damage. Also look for coolers that feature thinner profiles or thermostatically controlled, electric cooling fans.

Recommendations regarding fluid and filter changes for today's automatic transmissions vary from 60,000 to 100,000 miles in most pickups and SUVs under normal driving conditions. Under severe use, however, the recommendation usually drops to *at least* once every 60,000 miles—sometimes sooner. Severe use includes towing boats, even if your tow vehicle has a transmission cooler.

Temperature Gauge

A transmission temperature gauge is another useful piece of equipment, allowing you to monitor the temperature, and thus the health, of your automatic transmission. A few of the newest pickups and SUVs have them as part of the towing package—but most do not. That means you or a mechanic will have to handle the installation.

Installation of the sender unit varies considerably with the model: some install in the transmission oil pan; others replace the drain plug; and still others screw into a tapped hole (for example, the pressure-testing port) on the transmission housing itself. The wiring requirements are basic, although routing the wiring and neatly installing the gauge near your instrument cluster may be best left to an automotive expert. But it is relatively easy to install one on the A-pillar or on the dash using aftermarket mounting *pods* or brackets.

If you do have a temperature gauge and notice fluid temperatures rising, pull over and let the transmission cool down before it reaches the danger zone.

The A-pillar (between the windshield and the driver's side window) is an easy place to install a transmission temperature gauge.

Put the transmission in park, set the brake, and let the vehicle idle for a bit, which allows the fluid to continue circulating through the transmission cooler. Don't shut the engine off. This could cause the fluid to act as a heat sink, drawing heat from the transmission components, spiking the fluid temperature even further, and causing the very same damage you were trying to avoid.

TIRES

If you walked outside and checked the air pressures in your pickup's or SUV's tires, you might find that at least one is underinflated relative to the vehicle manufacturer's recommendations. Recent studies by the National Highway Traffic Safety Administration (NHTSA) and major tire companies show that 40 percent of light trucks and 28 percent of cars are driven with at least one tire at least 20 percent below the recommended tire pressure. That equates to the typical SUV tire being underinflated by about 8 pounds per square inch (psi) or more.

Problems

Low tire pressure affects your vehicle's safety and performance, the tires' longevity, and fuel economy. For example, driving around with four tires underinflated by as little as 5 psi, which is common on full-size pickups and SUVs, reduces your vehicle's fuel economy by more than 3 percent. Fuel consumption losses due to underinflation of up to 7 percent are normal.

From a safety standpoint, tires underinflated by as little as 3 psi can adversely affect vehicle handling—a fact brought to light a few years ago when underinflated tires were linked to a rash of fatal rollover accidents on some smaller SUVs.

Recent Goodyear and NHTSA tests show that when front tire pressures are below optimum inflation, a vehicle is harder to steer and requires more steering wheel input to turn. Braking is also adversely affected. The reports state: "Tires are designed to maximize their performance capabilities at a specific inflation pressure. When tires are underinflated, the shape of the tire's footprint and the pressure it exerts on the road surface are both altered. This degrades the tire's ability to transmit braking force to the road surface."

This has proven true in my own on-track emergency braking testing where a tow vehicle and boat trailer package were subjected to a full-on 60 mph panic stop. A tow vehicle and boat trailer with tires inflated to the recommended pressure stopped within a shorter distance, 10 to 15 percent shorter, than the same rig with tires underinflated 6 to 10 psi. The tow vehicle and trailer also tended to pull to the side of the underinflated tire(s) when hard braking was initiated.

Underinflation also increases the chances of hydroplaning on wet roads. Tires with lower-than-recommended air pressures tend to trap water and actually float over the road surface instead of allowing the water to squirt out the sides of the tread, which is what allows the tire to stay in contact with the pavement.

Underinflated tires also degrade tire life by causing the edges to wear faster than the center of the tread face. In extreme conditions, an underinflated tire can permit so much sidewall flex that heat will build up and cause the tire to delaminate catastrophically—in other words, a blowout.

Solutions

Tire underinflation is so prevalent because tires are porous and naturally leak air. Not much—maybe 1 pound of pressure per month on average—but that persistent air loss, coupled with changes in outside air temperatures, can lead to severely underinflated tires. The problem, however, is easily corrected. Here's how to check tire pressure:

- Find your vehicle's recommended tire pressures. This is printed on a sticker on the driver's side door pillar or in the vehicle's owner's manual. Do *not* use the figure molded onto the sidewall of the tire—that number is the maximum safe inflation for the tire, not the recommended value for your vehicle.
- Check tire pressure when the tire is cold—in other words, before driving.
- Use an accurate tire pressure gauge to check the tire's pressure. Remove the cap on the valve stem, press the business end of the gauge firmly against the valve so that no air is escaping, and read the gauge.
- Use a pump to inflate the tire to the recommended pressure. If the pump has a built-in gauge or an inflation setting,

The air pressure specification on tow vehicle tires is not the recommended tire pressure for your vehicle.

A good gauge will give you an accurate measurement of your tire pressure. Kicking, feeling, or looking at the tire will not.

TOW VEHICLE SAFETY CHECKS

Check the following on your tow vehicle at least as often as recommended by your owner's manual, preferably even more frequently:

- Engine belts
- Hoses
- Engine oil
- Transmission fluid level
- Tire tread and inflation
- Brake fluid level
- Brake shoes or pads
- Parking brake cable adjustment
- Wheel bearings (especially if you immerse the rear wheel bearings when launching or retrieving)
- Flasher relay (install heavy-duty relay when towing; replace with normal-duty relay when not)
- Lights and turn signals
- Windshield wiper blades and washer fluid

don't rely on its accuracy. After inflating the tire, use your own accurate tire gauge to check the pressure, and top off or deflate accordingly.

- Replace the valve-stem cap. This doesn't hold the air in, but it does keep grit out of the valve that could otherwise keep the valve from sealing properly.
- Repeat the procedure on each tire.
- Check tire pressures at least once a month.

Whichever way you choose to monitor tire pressure, take another look at your door placard. Is there just one inflation pressure? Or are there two sets of figures: one set of inflation pressures for normal loads, and the other for heavy loads? If there are two, then you should adjust your tires' inflation accordingly. Boost the pressures before towing, but remember to reduce them to the normal levels when you're not. Assuming that you're not towing a trailer most of the time, your vehicle will ride more comfortably and handle better with the lower recommended inflation pressure. However, if there's just one tire inflation pressure, don't add more air pressure for towing.

CHECK YOUR HITCH

The entire trailer hitch deserves a careful inspection at least once a year—preferably before the boating season begins:

- Get under the vehicle and make sure that all of the mounting bolts and brackets are tight and free of rust.
- Scrub the hitch with a stiff brush to remove any caked-on grime, and examine the welds carefully for cracks.
- If surface rust is present, remove it with a wire brush or emery paper, then reexamine the metal to make sure it's sound. Prime and repaint with an anti-rust coating.
- Check the drawbar for bends or dents, and check its fit in the receiver. Make sure the locking pin is in good condition, and that the matching holes in the drawbar and the receiver are not ovalled.
- Take an especially careful look at the tow ball. Is the locknut tight? Is the ball still smooth, or is it worn or gouged? Check for any signs of bending or stress cracks.
- Replace the ball if you find any problems—it is an inexpensive but a critical link in towing safety. Remember to install the lock washer before the nut, and use a torque wrench to snug the nut down to specification. Always make sure the ball has a thin coating of grease before dropping the coupler onto it.

If you aren't sure your vehicle's draw-bar and hitch ball are in good shape, purchase new ones. A number of companies offer drawbars and hitch balls. You can even find kits that provide everything you need, such as the Draw-Tite Towing Starter Kit.

THE TRAILER

For such seemingly simple pieces of equipment, trailers need a lot attention: brakes, wheel bearings, bunks or rollers, winches, and more. None of these are difficult to care for, but the care is essential. The two most common sources of trouble are the electrical system and tires.

Trailer Electrics

The electrical system is almost certainly the biggest source of problems on boat trailers. Luckily, trailer electrics are rudimentary, so troubleshooting and repairs tend to be simple as well.

A towing starter kit includes a drawbar, hitch ball, and related hardware. (CEQUENT GROUP)

A frequent cause of electrical failures on trailers is the lack of a good ground. This isn't surprising since frequent immersion in water will corrode most electrical connections. In a properly wired, four-wire system, the white wire is the ground. If all of your trailer lights don't work, this is the first thing to check. (Well, make that the second. The first should be to check that the trailer's wiring connector is plugged into the tow vehicle's wiring harness.) Find where the white wire is attached to the frame of the trailer and make sure there is a good metal-to-metal connection there. If the connection is corroded, take it down to bare metal with a wire brush or emery paper. Make sure the wire-end connector is sound and refasten it to the frame.

If a single light is out, the problem is likely either a bad bulb or a bad ground at the fixture. Swap the bulb for one you know is good. If that doesn't do it, check the bulb receptacle for corrosion. Still no good? Remove the fixture from the trailer and ensure that the fixture has good metal-to-metal contact with the frame. Finally, if that still doesn't do it, the problem is somewhere in the wiring, either on the trailer or on the tow vehicle's harness or its connector. Use a test lamp to check current at the vehicle harness. Refer to the illustration on the next page for typical trailer wiring configuration.

To help avoid electrical problems, here are some simple, useful preventive measures:

- Coat all lightbulb contacts and receptacles with waterproof, dielectric grease before installing the bulbs. This will dramatically reduce the number of failures.

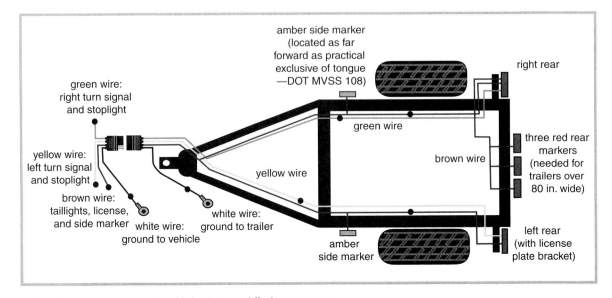

Trailer wiring systems are basic, and troubleshooting is not difficult. (CEQUENT GROUP)

- Search out every wire-to-wire connection on the trailer, and put a heat-shrink cover over any connection that's bare or covered with electrician's tape, duct tape, or a wire nut.
- Seal the electrical connection between the tow vehicle and the trailer before hitting the road. Wrap it with waterproof tape, or place the connector in a plastic bag and twist-tie it closed.
- When the boat's in your driveway or in storage, keep the connector contacts greased, and the connector protected by a plastic bag. Before your next trip, touch up the connector contacts with a fine file or emery paper.

Trailer Tires

Underinflation is the number-one reason for trailer tire failures, which take the form of premature wear or blowouts. A close second is mechanical damage caused by running over curb edges or off the sides of the pavement.

Unlike tow vehicles, boat trailers don't have door-pillar placards to tell you the recommended tire inflation pressure. Instead, a boat trailer tire's proper inflation pressure is noted right on the trailer tire's sidewall. Use whatever pressure is indicated to carry the "maximum load-carrying capacity" of

Driving even a short distance with a flat will thoroughly wreck a tire (and perhaps destroy the wheel, too). Proper tire maintenance is the best preventive measure.

that tire. In some boat trailer tires, this may be as high as 50 or 60 psi. Use an accurate pressure gauge, and don't try to guess the pressure by how the sidewall looks or how you think it should feel.

The same procedures for checking and adjusting pressure mentioned above for your tow vehicle's tires apply to your trailer's tires. In addition, check the spare's air pressure periodically—there's no sense carrying a spare around if it's flat. If you want to use a tire pressure monitoring system, you'll have to buy one just for the trailer, since most are limited to just four tires, and the tow vehicle's tires should probably take precedence.

Trailer tires and motor vehicle tires are built differently, so do not interchange them. Tire designations, which should be molded onto the sidewall of any tire you buy, include P (passenger car), LT (light truck), and ST (special trailer).

No matter how much you love a certain brand or look of tire on your tow vehicle, stick with an ST tire on the trailer. P tires have softer sidewalls than ST tires, and will allow the trailer to sway excessively while on the road. LT tires have stiffer sidewalls than ST tires and will cause a harsh ride that could beat up your boat. ST tires are, therefore, a compromise between car and light-truck tires, designed to be stiff enough to handle loads yet soft enough to absorb some road shock.

The tread pattern and internal structure are also different, given that trailer tires are never called upon to transfer forward-motion power to the ground, and the rubber compounds are formulated for different traction and longevity requirements. Another difference between trailer and tow-vehicle tires—and a real advantage, at that—is that trailer tires generally do not require balancing.

Trailer tires are identified by the designation ST, for special trailer (top). Tires for light trucks, like pickups and SUVs, are designated LT (bottom).

When it comes to buying new trailer tires, keep things simple. Stay with the same size that came on your trailer. Plus-sizing, or going to a bigger tire, can impose heavier loads on wheel bearings, causing them to wear more quickly. Larger tires may also interfere with fenders and may not mount properly on your existing rims.

Although radial tires are more expensive than bias-belted tires, they are a better choice for boat trailers, providing lower rolling resistance (for better tow-vehicle fuel economy); lower heat buildup and slower tread wear (for longer life); and a softer ride (imposing less stress on boat/trailer).

Trailer tires are compounded for excellent environmental resistance. Even so, trailer tires are more frequently replaced due to long-term degradation than to excessive wear, simply because most trailers get comparatively little use. Replace tires at least every five years, or whenever they show signs of age- or UV-induced cracking or delamination.

To prolong tire life to the maximum, block the wheels off the ground when the trailer is not in use for long periods, and cover them with heavy-duty vinyl tire covers to fend off UV rays. Alternately, remove the wheels and store them indoors.

Most jacks that come with cars, trucks, and SUVs will not work on trailers, so buy a small, general-purpose, scissors-type jack and a lug wrench of the proper size to fit the trailer's lug nuts. Make sure that the jack will go down low enough to fit under the trailer with a flat tire, and don't assume that your tow vehicle's lug wrench will fit the trailer. (If you have a really heavy boat and trailer, a hydraulic bottle jack may be needed to lift the weight, but clearance may be even more of a problem.)

If you do have a flat on the road:

1. Pull well off the road, onto a solid, level shoulder or similar flat area, and park the tow vehicle.
2. Loosen the lug nuts slightly while the wheel is still on the ground. If you raise the wheel first, the hub will spin as you try to loosen the nuts,
3. Once the nuts are free, jack up the trailer. If you can't get your jack beneath the trailer frame with a flat tire, place some firm, stable object just in front of the flat (a heavy block of wood, or even the spare wheel, will do). Then carefully drive the vehicle forward so that the flat wheel rides up on top of it. You should then have enough clearance to place the jack beneath the trailer.
4. After you've raised the trailer, remove the lug nuts, and lift off the wheel.
5. Place the good tire on the lug bolts. Hand-tighten the nuts first, then torque them down in an alternating pattern around the wheel. Do *not* tighten the bolts in consecutive order clockwise or counterclockwise. On a four-lug wheel, tighten in this order: 1 – 3 – 2 – 4. On a five-lug wheel: 1 – 3 – 5 – 2 – 4. Then repeat the sequence to make sure they're all tight.
6. As soon as you have the opportunity, get the flat repaired or replace the tire.

OTHER ITEMS TO CHECK

There are several other systems that every owner should inspect periodically and either fix, or have fixed, when necessary. And while this book won't turn you into a trailer mechanic, many of these items are straightforward enough for anyone with basic DIY skills. Others are best left to experts:

• Brakes: Boat trailers spend the majority of their time parked instead of being towed. Rust, dust, moisture, and other factors can wreak havoc on brake systems that are only used occasionally, so it is important to check the trailer's brakes both visually and mechanically before each trip. Look for obvious signs of trouble, such as leaking hydraulic fluid, frayed wiring, bad connections, and severely rusted brake housings. Make it a habit to test the brake system before hitting the highway: hook up the trailer and pull it slowly for a short distance (such as around the block or around the storage yard), applying the brakes at different levels of intensity. Many drum brakes have simple star-wheel adjustments, which you can easily adjust for excessive play. Before making the adjustment, however, check that there is sufficient lining material remaining. For surge brakes, check the level in the brake fluid reservoir at least once a year.

- Winch: Inspect the cable or strap and replace if damaged. Keep lubricated with grease. If rusted, sand and repaint. If you have an electric winch, check the electrolyte level in the battery on the trailer tongue. If the battery is not wired to be recharged by the tow vehicle's alternator, test its state of charge with a battery tester and recharge it as needed with a battery charger.
- Frame and suspension: Inspect all mounting bolts (axle, suspension, tongue, fenders, winch stand, etc.) for tightness. Inspect welds for cracks. Examine leaf spring and shocks for leaks and replace as needed. On steel trailers, sand off any rust and repaint frame and brackets.
- Tongue jack: Lubricate periodically. Sand and repaint as needed.
- Coupler: Inspect for cracks. Ensure smooth functioning of latch. Check level of brake fluid and top off as needed.

TOOLS AND SPARES

Most things that go wrong with a trailer while on the road can be readily repaired—if you have the right tools and spare parts. Keep a toolbox stocked with the items on this list, and throw it in the tow vehicle before taking off on a long trip:

- Replacement lightbulbs
- Electrical tools (test lamp, wire cutters, insulated wire, electrical tape)
- Extra flasher relay
- Tire change kit (spare wheel, jack, and lug wrench). If you have custom wheels with anti-theft lug nuts, make sure you have the appropriate key, wrench, or socket. If you put a lock on the spare wheel, pack the key in the tool kit.)
- Tire pump
- Spare towing ball with lock washer and nut
- Spare drawbar locking pin
- Bearing grease/grease gun
- Spare wheel bearing kit (bearings, seals, snap rings, etc.)
- Screwdrivers (slotted and Phillips)
- Hammer
- Adjustable wrench
- Snap-ring pliers (if needed for bearing installation)
- Extra tie-down straps
- Baling wire
- Duct tape
- Bungee cords
- Road flares

In addition, keep a small, all-materials fire extinguisher handy in the tow vehicle (and not in the toolbox, where it's *not* handy). It's not unheard of for a stray cigarette butt to end up on a boat's upholstery, carpeting, or canvas cover, or for excessive heat from malfunctioning wheel bearings to start a grease fire.

- Safety chains: Check for soundness. Replace S hooks with shackles or quick-links for improved security on the trailer tongue coupler. Check the bow tie-down safety chain for cracked or broken hooks and links.
- Bearings: Keep bearings filled with grease. Jack up the wheel and check for bearing play by pulling the wheel in and out on the hub. If you don't have bearing protectors, disassemble, clean, and repack the bearings with fresh grease annually. When driving on long trips, stop and check bearing temperature every hour or so. If they are too hot to keep your hand on, don't continue driving until you have resolved the problem.

- Bunks and rollers: Check brackets and mounting/adjusting bolts for tightness. Replace broken bunks and rollers and torn carpeting on bunks.
- Tie-downs: Replace worn or frayed straps.
- Tongue weight: Over the course of a boating season, the balance of a boat may be altered by the addition or substitution of various gear or (less often) its removal. At least once a year, check that the TW is between 5 and 10 percent of the trailer's gross total weight (GTW). Make adjustments to balance as needed.

A

Suppliers

BOAT TRAILER MANUFACTURERS, GENERAL

Boatmaster Trailers
12301 Metro Pkwy.
Ft. Myers, FL 33966
239-768-2224
www.boat-trailers.com

Continental Trailers
9200 NW 58th St.
Miami, FL 33178
800-432-1731
www.continentaltrailers.com

EZ Loader Boat Trailers
1462 Commerce Centre Pkwy.
Port St. Lucie, FL 34986
772-466-4185
www.ezloader.com

FastLoad Aluminum Trailers
611 West M.L. King Jr. Blvd.
Plant City, FL 33566
813-759-1889
www.fastloadtrailers.com

Float-On Corporation
1925 98th Ave.
Vero Beach, FL 32966
772-569-4440
www.floaton.com

King Trailer
3820 124th St. NE
Marysville, WA 98271
360-651-7887
www.kingtrailers.com

Loadmaster Trailer Co.
2354 E. Harbor Rd.
Port Clinton, OH 43452
800-258-6115
www.loadmastertrailerco.com

Load Rite Trailers
265 Lincoln Hwy.
Fairless Hills, PA 19030
800-562-3783
www.loadrite.com

Magic Tilt Trailers
2161 Lions Club Rd.
Clearwater, FL 33764
800-998-8458
www.magictilt.com

ShoreLand'r
102-122 East Hwy. 59 & 175
Ida Grove, IA 51445
800-859-3028
www.shorelandr.com

SAILBOAT TRAILER MANUFACTURERS

CastleCraft
P.O. Box 3
Braidwood, IL 60408
888-274-8490
www.castlecraft.com
Manufacturers of custom sailboat trailers for sailboats up to 14^1/$_2$ feet in length.

Loadmaster Trailer Co.
2354 E. Harbor Rd.
Port Clinton, OH 43452
800-258-6115
www.loadmastertrailerco.com
Manufacturers of custom sailboat trailers for sailboats ranging from 15 to 50 feet in length.

Long Trailer Company
2601 St. Andrews St.
Tarboro, NC 27886
252-823-8104
www.longtrailer.com
Manufacturers of custom sailboat trailers for sailboats ranging from 14 to 30 feet in length.

Sail-Trailers.com
6920 Macon Rd.
Columbus, GA 31907
706-888-6722
www.sail-trailers.com
Manufacturers of mast-raising systems and custom trailers for sailboats ranging from 8 to 32 feet in length.

The Sell Sail Corporation
16165 S. Hwy. 39
Stockton, MO 65785
417-276-5101
www.yachtworld.com/spurgeons
Manufacturers of custom sailboat trailers for boats ranging from 22 to 40 feet.

Triad Trailers
90 Danbury Rd.
New Milford, CT 06776
860-354-1146
www.triadtrailers.com
*Manufacturers of custom sailboat
trailers for boats ranging from 15 feet
to 41 feet in length.*

Trail "N" Sail
2240 Smokey Park Hwy.
Candler, NC 28715
828-670-8012
www.trailnsail.com
*Manufacturers of custom sailboat
trailers for boats ranging from 8 to 35
feet. Apart from a product list, the
website also features a boat measurement form for determining trailer
type/size and a list of state trailering
regulations.*

Tropic Trailer
9451 Workmen Way
Ft Myers, FL 33905
239-482-4430
www.tropictrailer.com
*Manufacturers of sailboat trailers for
boats from 8 to 35 feet.*

PONTOON BOAT TRAILER MANUFACTURERS

Eagle Trailer
300 Elm St.
Homer, MI 49245
517-568-5372
www.eagletrailer.com

EZ Loader Boat Trailers
1462 Commerce Centre Pkwy.
Port St. Lucie, FL 34986
772-466-4185
www.ezloader.com

Hoosier Trailers
115 E. Spring St.
LaGrange, IN 46761
260-463-3513
www.hoosiertrailer.com

Nationwide Trailer Co.
P.O. Box 968
Lebanon, MO 65536
888-262-2284
www.boat-trailer.com

ACCESSORIES MANUFACTUR-ERS AND DISTRIBUTORS

B&M Racing & Performance
Products
9142 Independence Ave.
Chatsworth, CA 91311
818-882-6422
www.bmracing.com
*B&M Racing offers performance-ori-
ented products, including heavy-duty
engine oil and transmission fluid
coolers (vehicles up to 19,000 GVW),
deep-dish transmission pans (extra
fluid equals lower temperatures), and
other related cooling products.*

Cequent Group
47774 Anchor Court West
Plymouth, MI 48170
734-656-3000
www.cequentgroup.com
*The Cequent Group is a leading man-
ufacturer, marketer, and distributor of
market-leading brands, lifestyle products, and accessories serving all
aspects of towing, including transmission coolers.*

Derale Cooling Products
3901 Medford St.
Los Angeles, CA 90063
800-421-6288
www.derale.com
*As the company's name states, Derale
Cooling Products specializes in all
aspects of cooling, including engine
oil, coolant, and transmission. Products include electric cooling fans,
clutch fans, transmission coolers,
engine oil coolers, power steering
coolers, frame coolers, transmission
pan coolers, and combination coolers.*

Extend A Hitch
22523 Byron St.
Hayward, CA 94541
510-733-3277
www.xtend-a-hitchnorthwest.com
*Manufacturers of trailer tongue
extensions.*

Flex-a-Lite
P.O. Box 580
Milton, WA 98354
800-851-1510
www.flex-a-lite.com
*For over 36 years, Flex-a-Lite has
been known as a manufacturer of
quality, high-performance belt-driven
and electric-engine cooling fans;
engine and transmission oil coolers;
and accessories. It offers a complete
line of products for automotive, light
truck, and heavy-duty applications.*

Gotta Show Products
P.O. Box 61
Laveen, AZ 85339
602-237-4506
www.gottashow.com
*Although specializing in the hot rod
and show car markets, Gotta Show
offers custom transmission cooler
hose kits that allow you to easily
build custom-fit hoses for any application. The hose has a stainless-steel
outer braid with an aircraft-quality
Teflon inner liner for high-temperature and abrasion resistance.*

Hayden Automotive
1241 Old Temescal Rd., Ste. 101
Corona, CA 92881
951-736-2665
www.haydenauto.com
*Hayden Automotive has long been
known as a manufacturer of engine
and transmission cooling products,
from clutch fans to oil coolers and
transmission fluid coolers. It offers
models for nearly every heavy-duty
engine/transmission combination
currently on the market.*

Jet Performance Products
17491 Apex Circle
Huntington Beach, CA 92647
800-535-1161
www.jetchip.com
While Jet Performance specializes in using computer technology to improve engine and shifting performance, they also offer a line of deep-dish transmission pans for Dodge, Ford, and GM applications.

Moroso Performance Products
80 Carter Dr.
Guilford, CT 06437
203-453-6571
www.moroso.com
Moroso has been making race-proven performance products for over 35 years. They offer a heavy-duty transmission cooler designed for high-heat race applications that can be installed on a variety of vehicles, including light trucks used as tow vehicles.

Northern Factory Sales, Inc.
2701 4th Ave. SW
Willmar, MN 56201
800-328-8900
www.northernfactory.com
This Minnesota-based company has been manufacturing radiators and transmission coolers for over 30 years. They offer products for agricultural, heavy-duty truck (semi), and racing applications, as well as coolers to fit most cars, pickups, and SUVs.

Perma-Cool
400 S. Rockefeller
Ontario, CA 91761
909-390-1550
www.perma-cool.com
One of the industry leaders in engine fluid cooling, Perma-Cool offers a complete line of light- and heavy-duty transmission coolers, engine oil coolers, and power steering fluid coolers. Also available are frame rail coolers, gauges, electric fans, remote oil thermostats, and other accessories vital to lowering operating temperatures on tow vehicles.

TCI Automotive
151 Industrial Dr.
Ashland, MS 38603
662-224-8972
www.tciauto.com/products/cooling
With more than 35 years of experience with on-track and heavy-duty towing applications, TCI specializes in building automatic transmissions and related products, including a proven line of transmission and engine oil coolers, fan kits, and gauges.

B

Resources for Trailering Laws in the United States and Canada

Sources of General Information

www.boatus.com
www.nasbla.org
www.camping-canada.com
    towing_regulations_e.htm
www.roadmasterinc.com
www.recvehicle.com/laws.html
www.americanboating.org/
    towing.asp
www.aamva.org

UNITED STATES

Alabama

www.dps.state.al.us
www.dot.state.al.us
www.dcnr.state.al.us

Alaska

www.state.ak.us/local/akpages/
    ADMIN/dmv/
www.alaskaboatingsafety.org

Arizona

www.azdot.gov

Arkansas

www.arkansashighways.com
www.arkansas.gov/dfa/motor_
    vehicle
www.agfc.state.ar.us

California

www.dmv.ca.gov
www.dbw.ca.gov

Colorado

www.revenue.state.co.us/mv_dir/
    home
parks.state.co.us/boating

Connecticut

www.ct.gov/dmv
www.dep.state.ct.us

Delaware

www.dmv.de.gov
www.dnrec.state.de.us/fw/
    fwwel.htm

District of Columbia

www.dmv.washingtondc.gov
www.mpdc.dc.gov

Florida

www.hsmv.state.fl.us
www.myfwc.com

Georgia

www.dds.ga.gov
www.goboatgeorgia.com

Hawaii

www.dmv.org/hi-hawaii/
    department-motor-vehicles.php
hawaii.gov/dlnr/dbor

Idaho

www.itd.idaho.gov
www.idahoparks.org

Illinois

www.cyberdriveillinois.com
www.dnr.state.il.us

Indiana

www.in.gov/bmv
www.in.gov/dnr

Iowa

www.dot.state.ia.us
www.iowadnr.com

Kansas

www.ksrevenue.org/vehicle.htm
www.kdwp.state.ks.us

Kentucky

www.kytc.state.ky.us
www.fw.ky.gov

Louisiana

www.dmv-department-of-motor-
    vehicles.com/LA_Louisiana_
    dmv_department_of_motor_
    vehicles.htm
www.wlf.louisiana.gov

Maine

www.state.me.us/sos/bmv
www.mefishwildlife.com
www.maine.gov/dmr

Maryland

www.mva.state.md.us
www.dnr.state.md.us

Massachusetts

www.mass.gov/rmv
www.mass.gov/dfwele/dle

Michigan

www.michigan.gov/sos
www.michigan.gov/dnr

Minnesota

www.dot.state.mn.us
www.dnr.state.mn.us

Mississippi

www.mdot.state.ms.us
www.mdwfp.com

Missouri

www.dor.state.mo.gov/mvdl
www.mswp.dps.mo.gov

Montana

www.mdt.mt.gov
www.fwp.state.mt.us

Nebraska

www.dmv.state.ne.us
www.ngpc.state.ne.us/boating

Nevada

www.dmvnv.com
www.ndow.org/boat

New Hampshire

www.nh.gov/safety/dmv/
www.nh.gov/safety/ss/index.html

New Jersey

www.nj.gov/mvc
www.state.nj.us/lps/njsp

New Mexico

www.tax.state.nm.us/mvd/mvd_
    home.htm
www.emnrd.state.nm.us/PRD/
    index.htm

New York

www.nydmv.state.ny.us
www.nysparks.com

North Carolina

www.ncdot.org/DMV
www.ncwildlife.org

North Dakota

www.dot.nd.gov
www.gf.nd.gov

Ohio

http://bmv.ohio.gov
www.dnr.state.oh.us/watercraft

Oklahoma

www.oktax.state.ok.us/mvhome
www.okladot.state.ok.us
www.dps.state.ok.us

Oregon

www.oregon.gov/ODOT/DMV
www.boatoregon.com

Pennsylvania

www.dmv.state.pa.us
www.fish.state.pa.us

Rhode Island

www.dmv.ri.gov
www.dem.ri.gov

South Carolina

www.scdmvonline.com
www.dnr.state.sc.us

South Dakota

www.state.sd.us/dps/dl/
www.sdgfp.info/index.htm

Tennessee

www.tdot.state.tn.us
www.state.tn.us/twra

Texas

www.dot.state.tx.us
www.tpwd.state.tx.us

Utah

http://driverlicense.utah.gov
www.stateparks.utah.gov

Vermont

www.aot.state.vt.us/dmv
www.dps.state.vt.us/vtsp/rec_
    enforce.html

Virginia

www.dmv.state.va.us
www.dgif.virginia.gov

Washington

www.dol.wa.gov
www.parks.wa.gov

West Virginia

www.wvdot.com
www.wvdnr.gov

Wisconsin

www.dot.state.wi.us
www.dnr.state.wi.us/org/es/
    enforcement/safety/boatsaf.htm

Wyoming

http://dot.state.wy.us
gf.state.wy.us

Puerto Rico

www.drna.gobierno.pr

Virgin Islands

www.dpnr.gov.vi

CANADA

Alberta

Maximum dimensions for trailer:
41'L × 5'6"W × 12'6"H (12.5 × 2.6 × 3.85 m)
Maximum length with trailer:
66 feet (20 m)
Gross trailer weight requiring independent braking system:
2,000 pounds or more (910 kg)
Trailer equipment requirements:
Breakaway device: N
Registration of towed vehicle: Y
Proof of ownership: Y
Drawbar required: Y

British Columbia

Maximum dimensions for trailer:
41'L × 8'6"W × 12'7"H (12.5 × 2.6 × 3.85 m)
Maximum length with trailer:
66 feet (20 m)
Gross trailer weight requiring independent braking system:
3,086 pounds (1,400 kg)
Trailer equipment requirements:
When the in-tow vehicle weight is more than 1,909 kilograms/4,200 pounds, the unit must have a functional safety breakaway brake on the attachment.

Manitoba

Maximum dimensions for trailer:
41'L × 8'6"W × 13'7"H (12.5 × 2.6 × 4.15 m)
Maximum length with trailer:
70$\frac{1}{2}$ feet (21.5 m)
Gross trailer weight requiring independent braking system:
2,006 pounds (910 kg)
Trailer equipment requirements:
Towed vehicle must have a driver or be equipped with an adequate towing device (tow dolly, drawbar, and lift arm) that compels it to remain in the course of the towing vehicle.

Distance shall not exceed 16 feet (5 m).
Towed vehicle must have functional brakes when not connected to tow bar.

New Brunswick

Maximum dimensions for trailer:
41'L × 8'6"W × 13'7"H (12.5 × 2.6 × 4.15 m)
Maximum length with trailer:
75.5 feet (23 m)
Gross trailer weight requiring independent braking system:
1.5 tons

Newfoundland

Maximum dimensions for trailer:
41'L × 8'6"W × 13'6"H (12.5 × 2.6 × 4.1 m)
Maximum length with trailer:
75.5 feet (23 m)
Trailer equipment requirements:
Independent braking system not required.
The service brakes on a combination of vehicles must be capable of bringing the motor vehicle and a fully loaded combination of vehicles to a standstill at 19 mph (30 km/h) under the following conditions: (1) in straight line; (2) within 33 feet/10 meters from the point at which the brakes were applied; and (3) on a dry and level paved surface made of eight asphalt or concrete that is free from loose materials.
Special permit required if towed vehicle not registered.

Northwest Territories/Nunavut

Maximum dimensions for trailer:
41'L × 8'6"W × 13'7"H (12.5 × 2.6 × 4.15 m)
Maximum length with trailer:
80 feet (25 m)

Gross trailer weight requiring independent braking system:
exceeds 2,998 pounds (1,360 kg).

Nova Scotia

Maximum dimensions for trailer:
48'1"L × 8'6"W × 13'7"H (14.65 × 2.6 × 4.15 m)
Maximum length with trailer:
75 feet (23 m)
Gross trailer weight requiring independent braking system:
exceeds 3,969 pounds (1,800 kg).
Trailer equipment requirements:
All lights must function on rear towed vehicles.
Tow dollies require trailer plates unless towed by vehicle plated in jurisdiction exempting dollies from registration.

Ontario

Maximum dimensions for trailer:
41'L × 8'6"W × 13'7"H (12.5 × 2.6 × 4.15 m)
Maximum length with trailer:
75 feet (23 m)
Gross trailer weight requiring independent braking system:
exceeds 2,998 pounds (1,360 kg)

Prince Edward Island

Maximum dimensions for trailer:
53'2"L × 8'6"W × 13'7"H (16.2 × 2.6 × 4.15 m)
Maximum length with trailer:
82 feet (25 m)
Gross trailer weight requiring independent braking system:
3,300 pounds (1,500 kg)
Trailer equipment requirements:
The brakes must be designed and connected so that the brakes are automatically applied if one of the vehicles being towed breaks away.

Registration of towed vehicle: N
Safety chains: Y
Tow bar required: maximum
length 12 feet (3.66 m)
Light hookup: Y
Towing behind pickup
camper/motor home is permitted.

Quebec

Maximum dimensions for trailer:
53'2"L × 8'6"W × 13'7"H (16.2 ×
2.6 × 4.15 m)
Maximum length with trailer:
75 feet (23 m)
Gross trailer weight requiring
independent braking system:
2,866 pounds (1,300 kg)
Trailer equipment requirements:
The towing vehicle must carry the
necessary equipment for operating the braking system of any
trailer being towed.

Drawbar or other connections
required towing not
recommended.

Saskatchewan

Maximum dimensions for trailer:
41'L × 8'6"W × 13'7"H (12.5 × 2.6 ×
4.15 m)
Maximum length with trailer:
75 feet (23 m)
Gross trailer weight requiring
independent braking system:
2,998 pounds (1,360 kg)
Trailer equipment requirements:
In the case of a breakaway from
the towing vehicle, the brake
system must automatically activate the brakes without affecting
the brakes of the towing vehicle.

Yukon Territory

Maximum dimensions for trailer:
53'L × 8'2"W × 13'8"H (16 × 2.5 ×
4.2 m)
Maximum length with trailer:
72 feet (22 m)
Gross trailer weight requiring
independent braking system
exceeds 2,000 pounds (910 kg) or
one half licensed weight of
towing vehicle.
Trailer equipment requirements:
Tow bar and safety chains: Y
Length must not exceed Highway
Regulation Limits.
Brake lights and turn signals: Y

Numbers in **bold** refer to pages with photos or illustrations

United States Power Squadrons is all about boating information, safety, and enjoyment

United States Power Squadrons (USPS) is a private organization with 50,000 enthusiastic members interested in all types of boating—motoring, sailing, paddling, rowing, fishing, cruising, hunting, and water sports—in 450 squadrons in the United States, Puerto Rico, and Japan.

USPS is all about boating information and sharing experiences. Through our USPS University courses, books, guides, presentations, and seminars, we've been teaching safe boating since 1914. USPS members include experts from the boating world: authors of leading marine books, magazine articles, and guides; U.S. Coast Guard–licensed masters and captains; and participants of many boards and commissions on marine topics worldwide. USPS members and the public enjoy courses created and taught by our volunteer instructors, at very reasonable costs. Course and seminar topics include:

- Basic Boating
- Seamanship
- GPS
- Coastal and Inland Navigation
- Understanding and Using Charts
- Offshore Navigation
- Celestial Navigation

- Marine Weather
- Marine Electronics
- Marine Engine Maintenance
- Cruise Planning
- Sailing
- Instructor Development
- Boat Handling

- VHF & Marine Radio
- Anchoring
- Marine Radar
- Marine Knots
- PaddleSmart™
- Boat Operator Certification

Members place a high value on fellowship through social events and civic service. Our members actively participate in the boating community through education, vessel safety checks, and a cooperative program with the National Oceanic and Atmospheric Administration (NOAA) to update navigation charts. USPS even maintains a network of port captains who provide expert local information for visiting boaters.

Perhaps the greatest benefit of participation with the United States Power Squadrons is the enjoyment, camaraderie, and opportunity to share experiences and ideas with other members, and to help the boating public. United States Power Squadrons endeavors to make boating a safer, more enjoyable experience for everyone. To learn more, visit www.usps.org.

Look for these other USPS Guides:

The Boatowner's Guide to GMDSS and Marine Radio
Celestial Sight Reduction Methods
Knots, Bends, and Hitches for Mariners
The One Minute Guide to the Nautical Rules of the Road
Marine Amateur Radio